CW00434457

CONTENTS

"...AND JUSTICE FOR ALL"

*How Lawyers Have
Derailed Justice in America*

BRADLEY M. LOTT

ISBN 978-1-0980-1994-5 (paperback)
ISBN 978-1-0980-1996-9 (hardcover)
ISBN 978-1-0980-1995-2 (digital)

Christian Faith Publishing, Inc.
832 Park Avenue
Meadville, PA 16335
www.christianfaithpublishing.com

Illustrations by Kristin C. Anderson

Printed in the United States of America

This book is dedicated to my parents, Bradley and Dorothy who instilled in me an unwavering sense of integrity and social justice through their own example and daily teachings.

INTRODUCTION

Societal Flaws Make for Divisive Consequences!

For too long, I have watched the evening news with depressing results. I have complained about this 24/7, recycled chatter, without stepping up and offering to do something about it. Our divisive societal flaws are regurgitated over and over, with only some superficial facts changing in the story. Beginning at the highest levels of our government, the misbehavior, criminal behavior, deceptive behavior, and self-serving behavior are all apparent in a moment's review of the current social landscape. Where does one begin to understand what this all means? Each news outlet has a different opinion and spin...maybe that's part of the problem. Do we actually need to be told what to think? And who is going to tell us…the dressed-for-attention announcer whose principal qualifications are good speech and, of course, good looks?

I began to look at the commonalities of the stories, be they financial, legal, political, or otherwise. In addition to the obvious "reporting" commonalities, I found another deeper commonality, and I wanted to know more about the "why." I inadvertently stumbled upon the "who" as well. This all came during a period of years when I had the unfortunate experience of divorce, robbery, and a substance abuse case against a family member…all involving the justice system. I don't want this book to be read as a tragedy; rather, I would like for my personal revealed experiences be anecdotal evidence and a step toward my more general observations across a much wider swath of the ills of our society…all with a common root cause.

We all have some level of preconceived beliefs, bias, and prejudice. I am no different and this writing may show that I have a soft spot for those who cannot fend for themselves and a disdain for those who seek to take advantage of the weak. But I believe that I am in good company with the vast majority of people in this great nation who believe the same. My intent is not to pick a fight over any specific issue; rather, my intent is to draw attention to and encourage a call to action in solving a problem of untruthfulness which leads to injustice in all aspects of our society. I don't profess any expertise in this area, and I am offering mostly anecdotal evidence drawn from personal experiences. That leaves my work open for valid criticism and I understand that. Nonetheless, if it will initiate discussion that leads to action, mission accomplished. Truth and justice must prevail. Justice through truth must become the cornerstone of our new view of society.

There are some parts of the Constitution, the Preamble, the Pledge of Allegiance, and the Bill of Rights that we all remember from having to accomplish the rote memorization in civics class. Of import to this writing are: "We the people," "One nation under God," and, "And justice for all." These three simple phrases from our important national documents impact our lives daily.

In looking at the issues reported daily, I noted quickly that "We the people" were routinely...absent. The issues are all about the special interest groups and the corresponding government or corporate bureaucrats. Where are the people on these issues, and why are we not energized to influence the action according to what "we the people" want? I was equally struck by the issues as having a basis in not just the touted rule of law, but in basic human decency...the kind that we learned about in Sunday school as children!

The Founders certainly envisioned the nation as being "one nation under God" and all that that simple phrase implies!

Lastly, and all too often, I hear the fairness of justice being questioned. I think that this is the most prevalent common denominator in the evening news and the one that causes the most personal pain to our fellow citizens...we, the people! Justice in all sectors of society is a distant hope as untruthfulness dominates the process in those sectors.

We will look at some social issues and see if we can confirm a common denominator as to a root cause or at least a thread of commonality of aggravating conditions. From the initial contact with the justice system, through public servant misbehavior, and all the media, business experiences, and political rhetoric, the common thread seems to be untruthfulness.

Most of us, as parents, have had to ferret out who really had the toy first because each child had a version of the story. Life is no different, except that we are all honest and have all learned to tell the truth…if you believe that, there is a lawyer out there who can spin your story as a "carved in stone footnote to the Ten Commandants" and do so with a straight face! Bring cash.

I posit that lawyers are that common denominator in the foundation of untruthful behavior and that their propensity to lie is what creates many of the inequalities in our society, especially those dominated by lawyers. Lawyers are trained to an adversarial system where a zealous advocacy in a case may, probably will, include weaving a story that is essentially false from crafted facts that may be true. In social parlance…a lie. In a lawyer's world…just advocating for his client. Please understand that this is the bread and butter of the profession of law… lawyers don't get paid to find truth or to achieve justice, they get paid to advocate and win for their client regardless of the cost. And that includes prosecutors, corporate, government, and personal lawyers.

At the core of the adversarial system, is the quest for victory and that alone seems to supersede the quest for truth and justice. Katherine Kruse wrote in an essay for the Nevada Law Journal that "the legal profession might be plagued by excessive lawyerly zeal that diverts lawyers away from the multiple dimensions of clients' problems and larger questions of justice: *winning at all costs serves the financial and reputational interests of lawyers."*

An argument presented by Judge Simon H. Rifkind, as presented in *The Lawyer's Role and Responsibility in Modern Society*, states, "In actual practice the ascertainment of the truth is not necessarily the target of the trial, [and] that values other than truth frequently take precedence." If the cost of representation doesn't preclude justice, then the necessity of victory surely will. Lawyers are not obligated to reveal what they know about the facts even if those facts would assure justice...they can withhold evidence in the interest of winning! That is what gives lawyers a very cloudy, self-defined concept of client confidentiality that all too often resembles the concealing of facts that might otherwise lead to justice! Professor John Humbach wrote in his review of *An Affair of State* by Richard Posner that there is a "serious discrepancy that exists between the standards of honesty that lawyers apply to themselves and those that the public expects of honest people in general and of a legitimate system of law in particular."

I'll suggest that the discrepancy to which Professor Humbach refers is actually a chasm of difference in society. That chasm is illuminated in the social discourse over justice and fairness.

As I prepared for this work, I read many articles and books about ethics, lawyers, and the intersection of the two. There are many, many good lawyers who are calling for change. Their call is probably out of earshot of the average person, like me, and therefore will not be heard or acted upon by "we the people." We will have to trust the lawyers to hear this message and act accordingly.

As I entered college over a half century ago, I was fascinated with the study of law…not that I had any aspiration of being a lawyer, but because the law was so logical, so precise, and so predictable. I was not a good student, ever, but I was an outstanding student in my pre-law classes because I was so enthralled with the subject matter.

Later, at Harvard's Kennedy School of Government, I was again captivated by the study of law when the Harvard Law School professors would teach a class in our curriculum. They were magnificent, and I was again reminded how logical and precise the law is. I have several friends who are honest, decent lawyers, and who will be very disappointed in reading my version of justice in America and its causes. My own granddaughter is in her first year of law school, and I know that this book will present some challenges to her, but she is strong, and I trust that my friends and family will know that I am simply standing up for what's right…justice for all. My vision of the law remains pure, but there is a horrible stain on the law that needs to be removed.

Those who disagree with me will become a source of learning for me. I am open to hearing the other side and perhaps changing my beliefs; however, I do find the juxtaposition of the adversary-advocate concept and ethical behavior to be a moot argument. If a lawyer cannot present his case within the accepted societal norm for ethics and truthfulness, then he needs to change his strategy for presentation. There is simply *no* room for elastic ethics in our courts, legislatures, boardrooms, and media outlets! Pursuit of truth and justice must supersede any and all notions of win/lose at the expense of truth and justice. No doubt this will generate a tirade of complaints from the legal world, but as the saying goes, "The first chicken to squawk…"

People all have varied experiences with justice in our society, but one thing is clear and that is that few are satisfied… except the lawyers who are mostly content. Those who are not satisfied are the good guys!

My real alert came during my divorce proceedings, where I was introduced to the cloudy world of American justice. My attorney was an Eagle Scout! He is a friend. He is a decent, upstanding gentleman. He is completely out of his element in the murky world of lawyers! There are many lawyers like him, but they are outnumbered by those who are just the opposite of him. My ex's attorney, by contrast, was a slippery, fact ignoring, blatantly dishonest, run-of-the-mill lawyer who you can find slinking around the courthouse or hawking his business and passing out business cards at the hospital ER. I was stunned by the tactical shenanigans that he performed; but more astonishingly, I was shocked by what the court tolerated. His legal modus operandi was (and remains) to overwhelm the opposition with motions, subpoenas, allegations, and delays. He submitted over two hundred subpoenas in the initial round, including demands to large banks that they turn over financial records of all clients of a family member who was a licensed financial broker. In court, he "stated," without admonition from the court, some of the most ludicrous things that one could imagine…he told the courtroom full of people that I owned a multibillion dollar, publicly traded, Canadian company! Lawyers often make references to weaving a story that is essentially false from crafted facts that may be true and this is an example.

The judge sat mute. I was stunned. My attorney assured me that this was not the time to object. That sets the stage for further examination, which we will do later.

In yet another encounter with the justice system, I turned to that system for help after a robbery at my business. I owned a manufacturing company that had recently bought out another company, and then hired its former owner as a consultant for design engineering. This is not an unusual practice. A year into the operations under my roof, the former owner decided that he was unhappy and wanted out of the deal…after having accepted all the benefits of the deal. In fairness, he was a full-blown alcoholic and addict and undergoing all the difficulties that are attendant to that disease.

Nonetheless, he entered the plant late on a Saturday night and backed trucks and trailers into the bays, and he and his accomplices stole all the work in progress, the inventory of finished products, the inventory of materials, the customer records, and most of the tools and machinery. We did not discover the loss until Monday morning, when the first shift arrived for work.

The police were able to nail down the facts pretty quickly, including the statement of a neighboring police department officer who encountered the thieves at a gas station where they offered to sell him some of the stolen goods! The reports and complaints were presented to the county prosecutor, along with binders of information listing serial numbers, pictures, supplier purchase orders and receipts, equipment inventory, and employee statements. The prosecutor gave the case a very low-level review and surmised in less than an hour that this was a case of a disgruntled employee, and therefore, a civil case. Two years and nearly a quarter of a million dollars in attorney's fees later, a civil court judge found that the loss was attributable to an identified "thief in the night" and that the police and prosecutor were negligent in their duties and that the insurance company was liable for their policy limits.

Today, four years later, the case has not been reconsidered by the prosecutor. Why would a prosecutor turn down such an obvious case? This will be further explored later in the book.

My final personal encounter with the justice system came as a family member was charged with DUI on three occasions over a period of ten years. I can provide no defense for the actions that resulted in the DUI, but I did get an eye-opening into the justice system as I sat in court and observed. I watched as lawyers quickly and mechanically moved through their obligatory statements and processes usually to the complete and utter astonishment of the poor soul standing in the orange jumpsuit, with their attorney whispering to them when to say yes and when to stand quiet. The system was machine-like efficient...

no dissent, no questions, and little justice! This entire despicable process will be the subject of more revelation later.

The NFL kneeling thing, as inappropriate and ill-advised as it was, is the canary in the coal mine of things to come.

After retiring from a thirty-four-year career in the US Marine Corps, I established a small business and began to work with my new colleagues in the business world. Of course, I understood and accepted that most of them were driven by the profit motive, and soon found that they knew little of true teamwork, true loyalty, and true integrity. They were not bad people, just different from those with whom I had served for the past thirty-four years. I was, however, struck by the blind trust that they placed in the justice system and the lawyers that ran it.

More than once, I found myself toe-to-toe with a lawyer who was designated to deal with me. These were, for the most part, just talkers. But, like hyenas, their strength was in their cackle. If the conversation left the boardroom and headed for the courtroom, the balance of power shifted quickly to the lawyer. But why? Is there not justice in the courtroom? I submit that as a rhetorical question at best…a serious condemnation of our society at worst.

Let there be no doubt that what justice is available in a courtroom is usually very expensive.

Over the next twelve years of civilian experience, I witnessed more and more the influence of this singular profession than I wanted to. I became more attentive to the involvement of lawyers and more judgmental of their perceived contributions

16

to business, politics, justice, or society in general, as opposed to their actual drag on the efficiency of society. I have selected a few areas from which I have drawn anecdotal evidence and from which to launch a more in-depth investigation. I'm not sure where this will take me, but surely, it will include more than is apparent on this initial list!

My format for this book includes a chapter of recommendations. I will attempt to give a hint of the recommendations at the end of each chapter, but I found that a summary of recommendations was more effective because they seem to be intertwined between subjects.

The bottom line is that we the people have to get involved and demand justice in all aspects of society.

These societal flaws have serious consequences and "justice for all," or the absence thereof, is the greatest of all. I'll kneel for that.

1

POLITICS

There Is No Justice in This Town

Political turmoil in our country is raging and nearly everything has become bifurcated along theoretically ideological paths. I say theoretically because I am suspicious of the level of political sophistication of many, if not most, of those who ascribe to an ideological party. Too many of our citizens have been told for too long that they are traditional members of a certain party; therefore, the bifurcation becomes blurred and sometimes dynamic. The discussions should be amongst the people, but instead, they are litigated for months, often engaging consulting law firms all for the purpose of crafting the message in support of the sponsor (read that as a *donor*).

The *crafting* seems to have no moral limits. The slightest intellectual rigor quickly reveals the obvious distortions, misinterpretations, misrepresentations, spin...*lies*. The midterm elections of 2018 were vicious, hard-fought, and well-funded...all of which brought out the worst in our political system.

In the end, the American people spoke in droves of voters and, as a body, seemed to have spoken logically. Perhaps the beginning of the end of the bifurcation is coming into sight.

But in the meantime, we have to deal with the fact that our political system is infected with lawyers and their lies. Look at the allegations against our current and recent past national leadership. Now look at the educational background of those involved in the most recent shenanigans...alleging and alleged against! Lawyers, lawyers, lawyers! Over half of all of our Presidents have been lawyers. Of those, the preponderance has been of the liberal party. *The Mueller Report* is a prime example of the shameful public discourse used by all parties to claim that the report supports their agenda.

Sort out the players. Most of the verbal sniping is being done by lawyers who can't agree on even the simplest aspects of the investigation, alleged crimes, or the meaning of the words in the report. What they all have done is to rile up the media into frenzy all spinning the stories to support their chosen side. The American people are the victims. It's our money, our legislators' opportunity costs lost, our investigatory agencies time wasted, and the hundreds of hours of negative electronic media bombarding us. Where did this go so wrong?

Remember the IRS official who pleaded the Fifth and then refused to explain to congress why she behaved in a criminal manner...she is a lawyer. Her counsel was a lawyer. Most of the congressmen questioning her were lawyers. We the people have never gotten a straight answer! We are getting the financial burden of the aftermath of the investigation as well as her hundred-grand-plus retirement! The Clintons...lawyers. Our current President is embroiled in an ongoing investigation that is replete with lawyers on both sides who are all pointing fingers and shouting, "Liar!" For all their faults, I think that they, too, have discovered the root problem...lawyers lie! On and on and in both parties...lawyers. I watched the Congressional hearings on TV where the Department of Justice Inspector General, Mr. Horowitz, was questioned by the Congressional committee. I was disgusted by the process. The vast majority of people in the room were lawyers, and the process was then complicated by them being very partisan politicians. The questions, all prepared by the staff and most likely lawyers, were not aimed at achieving justice or finding facts. The questions were all designed for the purpose of establishing talking points for interviews and political gain. All prepared for a story that may be believable from facts that may be true! Mr. Horowitz, an attorney himself, was patient and professional but must have felt like a political piñata rather than a man who had done what appeared to have been a thorough job of investigating an issue.

Most politicians are practiced at the nuances of speaking without commitment, meaningful facts, or references. They are also usually very gifted at avoiding responsibility and deflecting it to another. Isn't it interesting to see how the new non-law-yer politicians speak? For the most part, I think that they are very uncomfortable not telling the truth, so they simply state the facts. But, predictably, it doesn't take long for the good ol' boys to round them up and 'splain how Washington works… go along to get along, or more precisely, go along to get funded!

In my first years in Washington, DC, I was told that I never had to answer a question; rather, I only had to respond to it. I found that to be repugnant, as did most of my peers. If someone asked me a question, I felt obligated to answer their inquiry. If the question was a matter of classified material or if I did not have the authority to answer the question, I simply told them so. If the question was a stupid convoluted question to trap me into supporting their agenda, my response was deserv-edly simple and to the point. Marines are often complimented with a backhanded comment about being blunt, rude, and not politically correct. Yes, sir! We expect to tell the truth and hear the truth. If we are ever to solve a problem, how can we start with anything less than the facts? We used to have a saying to which I still subscribe: "Nothing is ever as good or as bad as first report."

Take a breath, ask some questions, and focus on the facts. A conclusion will fall into place. We should not let the first dramatic report skew our long-term judgment. Lawyers tend to stake out their ground first, design the facts that defend that ground, and then string those tailored facts together to make a believable story.

Politicians are always peppered with questions and expected to know everything of interest to every interest group in the country. A valid answer is that "I'm not aware of the details of that issue, but I will get back to you." But to a politician, he may have just exposed himself to the criticism of being unaware of important issues or, worse, may have lost a publicity opportunity to comment on something that will make him look smart.

Those risks are exacerbated by the leading and dishonest questions posed by the media. I think that we the people would be happy to hear back from our political leadership later if that would ensure that we got the correct answer the first time. Draw, shoot, aim rarely has a good outcome!

Political problem solving is much like setting up a word problem in mathematics. One needs to understand the facts individually and then as they relate to each other. If any of the facts are misinterpreted or misrepresented, the solution will be skewed to an incorrect answer...hence, why we end up with so many laws that bring your hand so forcefully to your forehead in exasperation! My father used to say, "Liars can figure and figures can lie, it's up to good men to be sure that they don't!" We the people are those "good men"! When laws don't make sense, why do we stand mute? For God's sake, we *are the people*!

Take the raging arguments about immigration. I am neither going to prosecute nor defend the issues; rather, I'll point out the absurdity of the arguments. It's all about posturing for interpretation by your intended audience. President Trump called members of the gang, MS-13, "animals" which was clearly in reference to their own motto and reputation for despicable violence. His speech word choice was to engender an emotional response against the gang violence and call people to action. Political opponents and much of the media went into a frenzy about the comment…not because many of them would or could defend the horrible acts of violence but because it was for political gain to do so. Truth had little bearing on the discussion. How can we even approach the solution of the problem of gang violence if we can't start with just the facts? We can disagree about the solution by expressing the value we give the various facts, but we can't just arbitrarily change the facts to fit our argument.

President Trump's comments were meant to convey his contempt for the behavior and reputation for the brutal acts of violence against mostly school kids. If the argument is to be that we should not denigrate anyone with the term *animal*, then that statement alone should suffice. After all, we should be focused on the elimination of the threats to our citizens by gangs in general and MS-13 in particular. The elongated arguments and obfuscations of the use of the term *animal* completely defused the effort to protect our citizens! Why would politicians do such a thing? Because their primary goal is to satiate the appetite of their base for opposition strikes! But why? Because their base votes and donates! Those donors may not represent "we the people" or support "one nation under God," so why do we not respond? They have the First Amendment right to speak and write even in their minority voice, but we the people have an equal voice under the same amendment! Please understand that the quest for power and wealth is clearly a goal of too many of those involved in politics!

We still have the problem of MS-13 violence. We have consumed endless hours of commentary and print about the merits of the word *animal*. We are more divided than ever. Who will take the leadership of the political community? Right now, it's lawyers because that's who we elect. And if you are a donor, that's who you pay to think your way!

I will confess to being a data hog. I have been charged with that many times, but I like facts and I especially like facts expressed in mathematics. Most lawyers don't like to deal with actual data. It's harder to massage them into stories than cleverly crafted words. Let's get some informative data in the public's eye!

I could not leave this section without some comment on the Judge Brett Kavanaugh confirmation hearing by the Senate Judiciary Committee. I will try to remain neutral as to my opinion of the confirmation recommendation itself and focus on the behavior of the committee members and their staff...all lawyers! In summary, I would say simply that they acted like lawyers...maybe 'nuff said. No, I have to comment on the horrendous behavior of all involved. *All* can be a dangerous word so I'll stick with *most* of those on the committee highlighted the art of the lawyer for all to see. They crafted stories which may or may not have been true from a series of truths and half-truths, all of which was done in the name of advocating for their particular person or interest. These were politicians acting as lawyers and the outcome was verbal vomit. There was no justice on this day! Senator Graham even admonished Judge Kavanaugh that there was to be no justice in "this town" at "this time."

I will take his comment to mean that he also logically inferred that there was no justice for the American people who were counting on these hearings to ferret out the worthiness of this nominee to serve on the Supreme Court. That hearing did nothing but disgust the American people. Each side claimed victory for their cause, but nobody claimed victory for "we the people"!

Our Founding Fathers wrote a constitution for the new republic through sheer brute determination that it be an enduring document intended to guide a government of the people, by the people, and for the people. They considered aspects of society then and into the future with the utmost clarity, but they failed to predict the dismal failure of the lawyers to mature along with the nation. Instead, the malignant tumor of the legal profession, hungry for power and wealth, metastasized to all aspects of our society, including our government of the people, by the people, and for the people. The demonstration of legal antics surrounding the nomination of Judge Kavanaugh to the Supreme Court was a national disgrace and will be a shameful reminder for us in the future. At the core of this disgrace is the universal untruthfulness wrapped in the lawyers' protective cloak of zealous advocacy and client confidentiality…lies and concealing evidence. The actions of lawyers acting like… lawyers.

In our constitutional purity, politicians are simply men and women carrying out the will of the people who elected them. In actuality, politicians are mostly careerists who start as lawyers and finish as whores. Politicians are viewed dead last in a recent Gallup Poll of Honesty and Ethics in Professions. They were in close company with car salesmen, who by the way, appear to be becoming extinct! They have earned their reputation as a body because the good haven't policed the bad, and we the people don't seem to care until it's too late.

It's high time that we vet the candidates, grill them in the campaign process, demand that they be held accountable for their actions, and personally accountable for their personal actions. We need to interrupt the canned speech and memorized talking points and get honest opinions from these candidates. Remember that the speeches and talking points are usually prepared by staff and a quick look at the staff of these candidates may tell enough to persuade the average person that they need to ask questions!

A wishful but unrealistic step one is to throw them all out and start from scratch. Justice begins with a just society of just laws. We will not find justice with this current crop of swamp dwellers. The problem is so pervasive that this is not a one and done action. We have to buckle up for rough couple of years as the swamp convulses and revolts.

Politicians and their political agenda will preclude the American people from getting the justice that they must demand. All the shenanigans (crimes) of the past few years appear to be headed for the closet without investigation or retribution because any action taken will be deemed as politically motivated, and therefore, off limits. That's nonsense! We don't need a politician to tell us what should or should not be prosecuted! We the people should be demanding that the President, the Attorney General, and the Justice Department do their job and prosecute the crimes that have been discovered regardless of the political liabilities. As for the politicians threatening "political repercussions" for the administration's prosecutorial actions, we need to hold them responsible at the next election…throw the bums out!

I watched an interview with the Gov. Matt Bevin of Kentucky and was fascinated by his commitments regarding politics, honesty, and term limits. This guy seems to be the personification of what the Founders had in mind. Kentucky found a winner here! There are more like Governor Bevin, but way too few. We need to find these good people and show our kindness and respect for their service, hold them responsible for their actions, and wish them well in their next vocation following a reasonable term of service! Career politicians are simply a liability. Career politicians trained as lawyers are the equivalent to nuclear waste…they are dangerous no matter where they go, other than encased in cement and entombed in a cave.

The 2018 midterm elections brought into focus the rising belief in the socialist party and their values. Two things leaped out at me. First, too much of the American electorate continues with its emotional rather than intellectual kinship with political ideas and politicians. Second, the rising stars of this not-so-new party (Soviet Union, Nazi Germany, Venezuela, North Korea, and Cuba) don't understand our system, much less the failures of the exemplified socialist experiments. We just elected a candidate to the US Congress who has displayed a complete misunderstanding of the legislative body to which she was blindly elected and an equal misunderstanding of the economies and societies of socialist countries.

So now we have an emotional electorate following a misdirected candidate…isn't that the blind leading the blind right into traffic? Where are the civics lessons that use to be required in high school? I don't want to become distracted by this problem of electorate education, but it does tie into what I am theorizing about dishonesty in so many aspects of our society. What is the fair and unbiased media doing to educate the electorate? Later in this work, I will discuss the media and the negative influence of lawyers in that profession as well.

I would be remiss if I left the discussion of Congress without comment on the very childish and very public spat between the President and the Speaker in January of 2019 relative to the State of the Union Address. The State of the Union report is a constitutionally mandated report. It has become a traditionally eloquent event of pomp and circumstance delivered verbally to a joint session of Congress in the House chambers attended by members of all three branches of government and broadcast on many electronic forms of communications.

In recent years, it has become a forum at which members or others could show their dissatisfaction with the President by not attending or sitting stone-faced in the audience. Both parties have equally disrespected the traditions and show of national unity over the years, and perhaps that is the new behavior that will become the tradition. That does not seem to be in the best interest of we the people, but it seems more like pouty behavior of a new generation of people arriving in Congress. Who are these people who are more about winning individually than winning collectively? Are these the children that we insisted all receive trophies in sports? And maybe, just maybe, they are mostly lawyers who function in a win-at-all-cost world.

The spat between the President and the speaker had a couple of elements. One was the opening of the government that had been closed (partially unfunded) and the other was the President's insistence on border security and funds for that endeavor. The State of the Union speech was simply a hostage in the argument over the budget. I communicated with my Congressman and asked him to remind all that we the people own the House, not the Speaker; that we the people are owed the State of the Union address, not the Speaker; and most importantly, our military members are asked every day to perform missions that might not fit their personal political positions, but they execute those missions because they took an oath to do so. That oath is the same as the oath taken by members of Congress...including the Speaker.

"I solemnly swear that I will support and defend the Constitution of the United State against all enemies foreign and domestic; that I will bear true faith and allegiance to the same; that I take this obligation freely, without mental reservation or purpose of evasion; and that I will well and faithfully discharge the duties of the office on which I am about to enter: So help me God."

Of particular import are the phrases, "I will support...the Constitution; I will bear true faith; I take this obligation without...purpose of evasion." That oath is absolutely void of party persuasion or personal beliefs. It is an oath that we the people trust will ensure that our will—the will of the majority of us—will be their mission. If ten lawyers each argued a position counter to that intent, they would each offer a persuasive argument by stringing many points that may have merit into a story that may be valid. That's their job. That's what we pay them to do. They craft stories that may be true from facts that might be true. But in the end, we do not achieve justice. In this case, members of Congress can justify not fulfilling their duty to we the people if they can string together the right interpretation of the Oath.

The Speaker of the House violated the Oath and let we the people down. Funding the government was a side show and a hostage that also let we the people down. Congress has abysmal public ratings for integrity, duty, and performance which are richly deserved.

In yet another affront to us, we the people need to be alerted to the encroachment into our election process by...lawyers. I was sickened to hear of the dozens of law suits in the mostly mid-western states for the purpose of re-districting the voting districts. Whenever this is done, it is gerrymandering. Perhaps the intention is to ensure that the districts evolve along with the population settlements, but I suspect an in-depth study would reveal that the actual purpose was to create favor to one party or the other. Neither party can claim immunity from this charge! But this new affront to the respectability of our election system is an effort by former President Obama and former Atty. Gen. Eric Holder. They have formed a group and sought donations for an effort to mount legal challenges to the current district lines…they are *suing* we the people to gain favor in the courts for their choice of districting. Lawyers are asking lawyers to decide for us!

We need the lawyers to take a break and let the American people make our own decisions. The infection of lawyerly manipulation doesn't stop there. The abomination of abuse in our election process was further demonstrated in the much publicized 2018 midterm elections in Florida and Arizona, where the lawyers moved into the space of shaping the outcome to meet the requirements of their client. We the people are *not* the client.

These election retrofit architects are not limited to only the media-focused cases; these jackals are operating all over the country. This is not a party phenomenon. Why in the world would we ever relinquish our elections to lawyers? Once the case is in the legal system, it will be completely determined by the lawyers…the legal system. The same herd of jackals that created the mess in the first place. The same herd of shameless crafters who can spin a story that is not true from a few facts that may be true. That should send a cold chill up the spine of all of us. Elections are clear cut and any deviation from the process should result in two actions.

First, the public official responsible for the breach needs to be held publically responsible. Second, those ballots involved need to be discarded. The potential for honest ballots to be discarded may be high (misplaced ballots discovered after the cut-off date but otherwise valid ballots) and these do need to be included, but the official responsible for custody from the balloting location to the counting location needs to be held responsible. There will be a few years of turmoil, but in the long run, we the people will take charge of our elections.

One final topic for this section is that of political party unity in deception. Either, both, or third parties are guilty of having done this, but the current team of Speaker Pelosi in the House and Leader Schumer and the current Democrat Party seem exceptionally adept in weaving a story that may not be true from some facts that may be true. None of this serves the people. We need to hear truth and then hear the political response to the *truth*. When the party dictates the story and talking points, we lose the input and perspective of the individual legislators.

I was pained to hear the story about collusion, then obstruction, but when the party rolled out their position on the economy, I was sickened. Never mind the political party, look at the economic facts and make your own decision. Each party will spin the economic news to favor their interests, but where does that end? Where do they just outright deceive us in order to win favor in an election? How about the truth? Justice comes in all aspects of our lives and truth from our elected officials is a justice that we deserve. If we can't discern clear justice from them...vote 'em out! Then find some non-lawyers who will tell us the truth.

Last in this chapter is a brief mention of the impeachment proceedings. I have listened with interest as each side promotes their position…was there a crime, were the documents drafted correctly, should there be witnesses, on and on ad nauseam. What is conspicuously absent is the mention, sincere mention not just window dressing for the argument, is justice! It seems to me that truth and justice have become victims, again, to the pursuit of a win by lawyers. Fact management is on display for the nation to see. One of the presenters even cited the lawyers, tactic that if you don't have a case, you can just proceed with obscurification through distraction, alternate interpretation, or long stories that may not be true woven from some facts that may be true. Just lies! What we the people should take from this very public demonstration of lawyers' perspective of justice is that we the people are at high risk for injustice. Just imagine, if such obvious injustice can occur on the national stage, how will you fare in a local court where the lawyers, judges, prosecutors, and defense lawyers all share the perspective on the impeachment crew! Our families, friends, neighbors, and fellow citizens are all at risk and only we the people can change this threat!

In the conclusion of this book, I will propose several ideas to correct the problems that lead to our political quagmire, but in the very end, we the people are responsible for Congress. We need to get involved in more that grumbling when things go wrong and we need to *vote* the bums out if they do not support the will of the people.

Senator Graham was correct…there is no justice in Washington, DC and I'll kneel for that.

2

LOBBYISTS AND STAFFERS

The Swamp Gets Deeper and Even
Further From Justice for All

There is an entire industry beneath the facade of Chiclet smiles and bad hair of the politicians. This industry of political consultants, lobbyists, media consultants, and fundraisers has become the hand that controls the legislative glove. If politicians are residents of the swamp, these people are the lowest sludge in the swamp. This industry is controlled and populated by a disproportionate number of…you guessed it, lawyers. Oh, by the way, one of the most active lobbyist efforts is the very liberal bar. They lobby against things like tort reform because a convoluted, over-domineering tort system keeps them in a lucrative business…at the expense of us. As mentioned, the American people hold this group of people in very low esteem. Yes, the swamp needs to be drained and dried by whichever party, or both parties, can make it happen. What are we the people doing to demand that? Very little. There are a few watchdog entities like Watchdog.org; Factcheck. org, PolitiFact.com, and OpenSecrets.org who are purported to be apolitical, but in the interest of just good due diligence are deserving of a through scrubbing of their political and ethical matrix. Meantime, their record and reputation is that they are as unbiased as we can find and they are available for most any government operations questions…we the people should avail ourselves of this wonderful resource.

In Washington, DC, there is a part of town with very plush offices, swanky eateries, quiet bars, and cafés in an area along K Street. These are the lobbyists. This is where you place your cash investment in the future of a particular legislative program. If you look at the principals, you will find past notables of congress and presidential cabinets on the boards and staffs of the lobbying firms. Here are the men and women with whom we entrusted with our nation's business, now sliding around in the shadows, selling their influence, and violating the trust that we once found in them.

Some estimates are that senators must raise more than $14,000 dollars a day in order to fund their reelection! Lobbyists stand ready to donate and organize fundraisers for elected officials in order to buy influence for their clients. The sleight of hand here is that the purchased access occurs in a social setting and does not have to appear as a meeting between the two…but the message is loud and clear! Another method of influence is to offer a job to the member today that will provide for his reward after he leaves office. This is known as "the revolving door."

In the past forty years, this practice has grown from 5 percent of departing members to today's 50 percent of senators and 33 percent of congressmen exiting to a job in the lobbyist world. Their pay can go exponentially up as they are rewarded for their loyalty and action. Even though there are laws on the books to govern the behavior of the lobbyists, including a required registration, many have dodged the requirements by serving as a silent lobbyist. Their influence, not just their name, is what's important.

Lobbyists will often offer drafted legislation for the members and staff in order to facilitate the intended influence. More times than not, lobbyists, at a minimum, review the drafted legislation and make recommended changes. In part, I understand that some legislation may need some technical review and advice, but when the laws are written by the governed industry…that's just reckless and negligent. Who would let the fox design the hen house as well as maintain the guard over it? Greedy, lazy public servants, that's who!

I don't have accurate figures on lobbyists, and I'm not sure that anyone else does either. Legally, they are defined carefully, but any two people can do an essentially identical job and yet be classified as either lobbyist or a consultant! Estimates are that there are between twelve thousand and fifteen thousand lobbyists in DC, but some estimate that there are actually closer to 100,000, including those in the shadows. There are only 535 members of Congress. Imagine a battle where the ratio was 200 to 1! Congressional members can be protected only by their own scruples and integrity. The good ones fight daily to fend off the endless assault by the brokers of influence. There is always a cost. That cost may require a concession or may result in a prized committee assignment, but those brokers are not going to leave without a deal unless they face a Jim Jordan from Ohio or a Paul Mitchell from Michigan who both represent their constituents with integrity and loyalty.

Remember that roughly half of the members of Congress are lawyers! Maybe the new breed elected in recent years will bring hope for integrity in office because in the past fifty years...or more...they have left a trail of societal destruction and retired wealthy politicians. President Truman drove his own car back to Missouri when he left office in 1952 and was proud to have served and to have retained his integrity and reputation. President Truman lived the rest of his life in rather humble settings and without any of the trappings of wealth and fame. The history books honor this great man. President Clinton, in contrast, departed Washington on Air Force One after absconding with a collection of White House valuables and having dodged an impeachment conviction...but today, his wealth is measured in the hundreds of millions...no integrity retained and his reputation in tatters. Bill and Hillary Clinton live an extravagant lifestyle replete with all the trappings of fame and wealth.

History will report the Clinton administration as an anomaly of American tradition but a forecast of the failures that await the nation in the future. This is a case study worthy of scholastic review, lest we repeat the same behavior with the same criminal results!

The fire of deviousness in these career politicians is fanned by the cadre of lobbyists and staffers who feed at the bottom for power and wealth for themselves. The notion that so many of these influence peddlers were at one time the trusted public servants for whom we voted is a sad commentary of our current political system. Lawmaking is very difficult work.

What motivates these people to come from their homes across the nation and settle into this swamp of depravity? Power, wealth, and notoriety are certainly an influence. One has only to sit in a DC area bar for a bit to hear the conversations amongst the staffers in attendance. There is clearly a pecking order as established by the announcement as to who one's boss is! After that comes the disgusting conversation of trades, concessions, and outright strong-arming that can be heard as they profess to be on the winning end of the deal-making. Winning here is much like lawyers winning in the adversarial system…truth and justice take a distant second place to the win! How could we expect anything different? Most of these manipulators are lawyers! Advocating for the win and concealing facts deemed harmful to their agenda, all at the expense of justice, are hallmarks of lawyers being lawyers and their trail can be followed much like a hunter follows the droppings of a coyote…it stinks.

Members of Congress and their staffs do not have the necessary technical background for the wide swath of industry that they represent, and therefore, lobbyists are probably a necessary evil, but with just a bit of integrity, they could fill the necessity without being evil.

The concept of justice for all is drowning in the swamp and I'll kneel for that.

3

GOVERNMENT
BUREAUCRACY

*A Story of No Accountability
and Therefore…No Justice*

The thrust of this book is about the absence of truthfulness in our society with the thesis that lawyers are at the core of that untruthfulness. One would hope that our trusted government bureaucracy would be immune from the dishonesty of politics but…not so! The much discussed "deep state" has horrible implications of an effort within the government to steer the government in an alternate direction of that which may not necessarily be the will of the people. Just the notion of this should be a chilling call-to-action to the people. The government bureaucracy is the structure that should support the three branches of government in the best interest of we the people as the result of our election preferences.

If you look carefully at the leadership and key staffing of these support agencies, you will find an abundance of lawyers. Here is a quick review of what our government should be doing to ensure that people feel secure and free to pursue their happiness.

Where do I start? Threats to our society are at all levels and all sides…some are foreign entities and efforts; some are homegrown criminals; some are simply greedy opportunists preying on the most vulnerable of society; some are those elected or appointed to serve us! What are we doing? Not enough. Cyber threats from outside our borders are being addressed for the most part by the NSA…remember them? The people who don't spy on Americans!

In the aftermath of the revelation of the domestic spying and the lies to cover it up came the believable story crafted from a few facts which may have been true. The story was presented as truth and served as a successful diversion and the nation gave little attention to the event. Congress holds the reins on the powers of these errant bureaucrats but has done little to ensure that they are doing their job or more importantly respecting the privacy of our citizens. Our most senior intelligence community leaders have lied to Congress without recourse and still retired on our dime. Now they have become paid commentators with the cable TV circus.

Greedy opportunists, like too many politicians, erode the confidence in the government's ability to protect us and make us feel safe. The opioid crisis was driven by out-of-control production by big pharma. Where was the FDA? Veterans were wait-listed for months to see a doctor and when the death list became too long, the VA simply lied about the wait times. We had a water crisis in Flint, Michigan, but the EPA was too busy policing the mud puddles in the western states and issues of beach incursion on the ocean in Florida to have found the Flint water crisis worthy of investigation. The IRS...just needs to be put out of its misery. We need a flat tax with no more than five deductions. The IRS has become so political that they cannot be trusted to handle the nation's tax collection. The downside is that if you eliminated the IRS, thousands of attorneys would be on the street and lurking for work. The list could go on and on.

The bottom line is that government is not doing a good job of making us feel secure or facilitating our pursuit of happiness. The government is doing just the opposite by condoning the bureaucratic misbehavior and abuse of power of our public servants, which just exacerbates the erosion of confidence of we the people in our government. The political right calls for more government authority to fully protect us from terrorism and the political left calls for less authority and intrusion to protect us from the government! Maybe the answer is adequately bridled authority that would ensure our safety and then take quick, transparent, decisive disciplinary action for those who violate the process and our privacy.

Every time I receive an alert to a potential misuse of a credit card or an obvious scam call, I wish for more security of our electronic lives. But then, I also wonder about the abuses inside our law enforcement and intelligence agencies and wish for more privacy! So I go back to the notion of adequate authority with the protection of enforced privacy. This is all about legislation, court review, and agency leadership…every step is contaminated with lawyers. So again, the first step may be to introduce an interrupting action where a civilian review board (no lawyers wanted!) drafts the legislation and oversees the agency implementation and enforcement of the new laws. The resulting process could become a habitual process in three to four years, at which time the review board could be retired! We can be safe and free at the same time.

In my career in the Marines, I learned and then experienced a very basic concept of a successful society…confidence in the government. As we were deployed to areas of trouble, the basic problem in rebuilding was first reestablishing trust with the people that the new government was there to protect and serve them. The other issues like war, food, water, and medical services were easy compared to the task of building trust. This example has pages of details, but what I want to convey is that if you look at the building of a society in reverse, you have the dismantling of a society.

First on the agenda of terrorists in dismantling a society is to create doubt that the government can protect and serve the people. Bombing a building, poisoning a water supply, crashing an airplane are, in and of themselves, of little threat to the overall security of the nation. It is the notion that the government has failed to protect us and the loss of confidence as a result that present the greatest threat to the nation!

Now let's think of what is happening at the three letter agencies NSA, CIA, FBI, and DOJ...all their issues of abuse have eroded confidence in the government. Trusted leaders have lied before Congress and the American people without recourse. The agencies have self-appointed themselves as being so important and so secret that they have the right to operate independently of the Executive and Legislative Branch, and I have little doubt that they would not respond truthfully to the Judicial Branch either...ergo, the FISA Court applications!

The enemies of our democracy must be delighted with the self-destructive nature of our own bureaucracy! The fix is enforcement of the laws and regulations that govern the agencies. Here is an opportunity for all the lawyers in the system to do the right thing and show the people that the government can be trusted. Through the many investigations, allegations, and whistleblowers, hundreds of implicated public servants as well as elected and appointed officials have been identified who need to be disciplined as having failed our nation through their own greed, bias, and criminality.

The entire notion of a shadow government, a deep state, or whatever name it may have needs to be dealt with so that the public, we the people, can regain the trust of our government. This effort will require an effort by all...from the President to the Congress to the media. This is for the good of the nation.

There has been too much talking. It is time to act! The news should be replete with stories of the cleanup of our government and the reestablishment of confidence that we are truly a government of the people, by the people, and for the people. And for those who failed in honoring the trust that we put in them, they need to be sentenced harshly. There should be no retirements, resignations, or transfers where there has been criminality. That only contributes to the loss in confidence that the American people have for our government.

Think of the young kid from a disadvantaged background standing before a court. Does he see his justice as being equal to the justice meted out to those high-level bureaucrats who failed our trust, or does he see an unequal system of justice? His young face is the face of our next generation. I don't have to draw the conclusion for you. Every reader of this book will say that if not themselves, then someone they know has been held to a stricter standard of societal behavior than the senior bureaucrats and elected officials who have the influence to dodge the consequences of their criminal actions.

I am both pained and offended by the long list of officials from the CIA, FBI, DOJ, and NSA that are not currently being investigated and appear not to be on track for accountability. We the people deserve to know what happened and who was held accountable for the misdeeds. We have at least two dozen high level bureaucrats who have dodged responsibility for very high level misdeeds while we have so many young people with far less affluent means who are being held accountable for much lower levels of crimes.

There is much posturing for the next election, but I have not yet heard a single pledge to clean up this mess. President Trump has said that he will "drain the swamp" but even his highest priorities are running into the knee-deep sludge of DC.

I would challenge every one of these wannabes to take a position on investigating, prosecuting, and cleansing the government. If they have the courage to make the commitment, we will have to hold them to their promise once they attain office. I hold no hope that anyone of them has the courage to take such a position. We will hear more unbelievable tales spun from a few truths…the product of their lawyer training.

As I write this, there are over two dozen announced candidates running for president. The vast majority of whom are lawyers and many of them are former prosecutors. A cursory scan of their public biography (not their campaign website bio) will lead to the swath of destruction that their past behavior has left. Remember, they are trained to win even at the expense of justice. Every time I hear them speak, I think of the young lady in the orange jumpsuit, pleading for justice only to be met with an "I won" smug attitude of the judge and prosecutor. Do any of us believe that they will change their behavior?

Without firm, transparent accountability, there can be no justice for the American people. I'll kneel for that.

4

MEDIA

Never Let the Facts Get in the Way of a Good Story. Justice be Damned!

We the people need a free and unbiased press to investigate all sides of the political quagmire and give us the facts upon which we can build our own opinions and form our own positions relative to a candidate, a politician, a proposed law, or a court's decision. We don't have that available to us today in a clear and unobstructed way.

The media is horribly bifurcated along political ideological lines...liberal/conservative with all the extremes. Before I give any credence to the stories that I read or watch on TV, I routinely look up the reporters/commentators, their guests, and supporting panels and am never shocked to find that, again, a disproportionate number are...lawyers.

Listen to their convoluted speech. Truth can be stated in a few words. A prevarication (lie) has to be crafted with the caveats of "Law Lies 101" such as "considering the many variables," "my sources have told me," "as known to many," and "as I understand." Nothing documented, just vague, artfully crafted statements that don't represent the real facts.

Why would a wannabe journalist go to law school other than to learn to word craft? Why would a lawyer become a journalist other than they have a skill that producers with an agenda need...word crafting? Remember the legal notion of weaving a story that is essentially false from crafted facts that may be true? That is a skill not taught in journalism school. One needs the post-grad experience of law school to learn that particular skill!

I understand the difference between reporters and opinion commentators, but the general public may not always see the difference as clearly, and therefore, give the commentator's pitch too much credit. What the public needs are declarative statements of fact as the reporters have discovered in their investigation. We need to hear reporters asking piercing questions that are not laced with bias. What happened to real journalists who are trained to ethically report? Why do we reward any of the yakking commentators by watching their broadcast? Lawyers consider "fact management" as a tool in their kit. Those who need false but believable stories created from some truthful facts are in need of some fact management and a lawyer…who better to report the news as the client wants it reported? This is not the free press envisioned by the Founding Fathers!

Thomas Jefferson cautioned us: "The only security is in a free press. The force of public opinion cannot be resisted, when permitted freely to be expressed. The agitation it produces must be submitted to. It is necessary, to keep the waters pure."

One hundred and fifty years later, Pres. John F. Kennedy reminded us: "Without debate, without criticism, no administration and no country can succeed—and no republic can survive."

I'm not sure that our Founding Fathers ever envisioned a time when opinions would surpass facts in the press. Opinions are important for sure, but before the public can evaluate an opinion, they need the facts. We are long on opinions and short on facts in our daily news cycle. The willingness of opinion commentators, their producers, and the ownership of the outlet to pawn off their bias opinions as news is a real question of integrity! Our adherence to the concept of "one nation under God" falls short when considering the notion that we are not "a false witness who breathes out lies…nor…one who sows discord among brothers" (Prov. 6:16–19).

On the contrary, that biblical reference sounds like a description of many of our news sources! If a lawyer's best skill to win a bad case is to confuse the judge and jury through obfuscation, then doesn't that skill transfer easily to the media? Of course. It's a natural progression leading to the demise of trust in our media. We need more true professional journalists and no more lying lawyers in our press corps!

Now, what happens when the press begins to side with one party or the other? Where are the hard questions that we the people need asked? If the press sides with the administration, then we risk not knowing of potential abuses, and if the press sides with the opposition party, then we risk simply stalling the government. Opinions are by definition, one-sided. Facts and fact reporting are free of opinion and of value to the side of good! Journalism schools, I'm sure, teach the pure version of the profession replete with attendant ethics. We need more of these graduates in the business of journalism and fewer word crafters and opinionated talking heads.

I treasure the real journalists and their reports. I despise those whose reports consider facts to be a nuisance in the way of a good story.

Margaret Sullivan, *The Washington Post's* media columnist, wrote an article in December of 2017 of her personal quest for the truth about the public opinion of the media. Her article was spot on. She may have started with an opinion regarding the health of her profession, but she never showed any bias. In part, her summary included this position and recommendation:

The country isn't, I believe, rigidly divided into those who will always hate the media and those who deeply appreciate us. As a result, I think it's more important than ever that we journalists continue striving to win over those who are skeptical, conflicted, or simply apathetic. We need to heed complaints about the blending of news and opinion, and to make it clear which is which. We need to focus more intently—and more engagingly—on subjects that matter most to ordinary people's lives, and to calm down about the White House intrigue and Trump's every tweet. And we need to stamp out the snarky attitude that seems to brag, 'I'm smarter than my audience.' Perhaps most important, we need to be much more transparent—willing to explain our work, and own up to our inevitable mistakes.

I can't find any better words to sum up the fix for the confidence-in-the-media problem than those in Ms. Sullivan's article. This author is a journalism graduate and proudly states her claim to be a watchdog for the American people. I salute that. We need more Margaret Sullivans in the media! If we the people are to trust our media to find the details, then the media needs to reassure us that they are guarding facts like a watchdog and sounding the alarm when needed.

As a result of my work on this book, I have gained a whole new respect for journalists...real journalists. I have read their Code of Ethics as published by the *Society of Professional Journalists*. I actually printed it and have it in my office. The American Bar would do well to read it! The SPJ has written a simple one-page "see Spot run" version of the book that the lawyers prepared for themselves which is not even titled as a pledge to ethical behavior.

The problem here is that not all print and electronic journalists are...journalists! They are something less. Something untrained as a journalist. I would like to see a subtitle on every article or every TV screen or announcement on radio and social media that recognizes the reporter as a professional journalist. That way I could change the channel or line the bird cage sooner! I have suffered the wrath of curious journalists and I didn't like it. The questions were hard and they accepted nothing less than a full answer. But I will fight a lifetime to defend their right...actually their duty....to find the details and report to the nation. Thomas Jefferson heavily influenced the Founding Fathers regarding the importance of a free press but between the times he touted their importance and his presidency, papers had become opinionated and he changed his praise to criticism of the abuses of the press in their skewed reporting.

Obviously, beauty is in the eyes of the beholder here! But we must continue to strive for a free, fair, and accurate press because that is what ensures the survival of our democracy. We need professional journalists who have pledged to abide by the ethics of their profession.

My message for the media management is: lose the lawyers and hire real journalists. Keep your opinions to yourself and give us the facts. We'll sort it out from there!

Facts should make the story and justice should be the outcome of a fair story. Absent truth, there is no justice and I'll kneel for that.

5

BUSINESS

Caveat Emptor—I Can Lie Better Than You Can Discern a Lie... I Win! Business without Justice

Small businesses are driven by their reputation for honesty and performance. They don't have the public relations departments or the legal resources to cover for their mistakes. They actually walk a social tightrope without a net as they balance their business. Their prices may be a bit higher, perhaps, because their consumer visibility is much lower than the big brands and their volume-purchasing power is lower. The internet is drastically changing all that. Amazon is changing that! Nonetheless, the marketplace is skewed toward the large businesses. Lawyers in business bring their stance on truthfulness with them and that's what perpetuates the old merchant's cry of caveat emptor. Businesses today cannot survive in the long run with that kind of deceitful approach.

I recently met with another small business for the purpose of conducting a buy/sell pass-through deal. We had discussed the deal by phone a number of times and this was the first face-to-face meeting. The meeting went well socially and we struck a deal. About an hour after the breakfast meeting, I got a call from the administration manager at the other company, asking if he could send over some papers for signature. Within the hour, I had a stack of CYA paperwork. The language was artful and convoluted, but it was obviously going to stall the deal if I pressed to change it. None of it was about the buy, sell, pass-through, or even pricing…it was all about the attorney solutions to the many events that might come up as a result of this deal!

We did not sign the deal and I will not do business with them again. Their attorneys had taken control of the business and subjugated a handshake to a stack of paper while empowering themselves in the process.

A respected friend of mine who is a lawyer and a very good one, advised me many years ago to never let a lawyer take charge of my area of responsibility or to ever tell me no. He was right then and his advice still applies today. Businesses today are increasingly held hostage by lawyers and their policies. There is perhaps no greater example of this than the pharmaceutical industry. Whether the angle is good treatments left uncirculated because lesser treatments have better profits; high risk bad treatments with high profit margins; or unnecessary treatments for ailments that could be treated with no drugs at all, at the core of the angle is untruthfulness.

Imagine if big pharma let their doctors speak rather than their lawyers! Imagine if we heard facts about the drugs and their potential and risks from a physician sworn to place his patients first! Profits would be down but quality of life would skyrocket! And we would no longer have to listen to the speed talker at the end of each advertisement…but then we probably wouldn't need the advertisements! Imagine where we could be if opioid-based drugs were controlled by just ethical sworn physicians and just for the purpose of short-term medicinal care. A lawyer in the medical field is truly putting the fox in the hen house! Between the in-house, big-pharma lawyers, the legislative lawyers, the American Bar and their trial lawyers, and the insurance lawyers, it's amazing that we aren't all dead by now just from lawyer overload!

Our national health care structure is dominated by lawyers, not doctors. Imagine how you'd react if you took your car for mechanical service only to find that the dealer's garage staff was dominated by hairdressers. You might end up with a well-detailed car that still won't run!

The cost of many products can be inflated exponentially by the shenanigans of the lawyers. Have you ever listened to the speed talkers citing all the applicable caveats to an advertisement? Probably not, but the company feels protected from you because they can claim that you were advised but failed to heed the warnings. If that ever got into a courtroom, the judge would have to rule on the validity of the speed talker's advice. Is there any doubt where the judge would stand? Is this what we the people want? We need honesty in advertising. Tell the truth about the product.

I understand that there is a certain amount of pride and professional puffery that surrounds a company's claims for its products. "The best in the world," "unbeatable at any price," "one of a kind," are examples of such advertising claims. I'd rather have the pure truth, but I do understand that manufacturers may just believe that they are the world's best. Okay, but to put tiny print at the bottom of the screen that cannot possibly be read that warns you that nothing has been tested and that none of the claims are supported by government agencies tells me that there is a lawyer crafting the words that will defend the lies of the advertisement. That is, defending the lies in a courtroom full of lawyers all being paid to out-lie the other. Why do we stand for this?

As businessmen, we tend to try to pass the legal costs along to the customer as much as we can, but there is a low tolerance for that in the case of low-volume production that most small businesses pursue. Many opportunity decisions are considered and rejected simply because of the legal issues surrounding it.

We have a client who owns a superbly capable engineering and manufacturing company. He will not consider many projects because he believes that the tort laws and lawyers are waiting in ambush. Many good ideas and projects never make it to market because of this founded fear. He does market many of those opportunities to the government with great success because of their indemnification policy. We are proud of the products that he has sold, but the American public should have access to the same good products.

In another encounter with big business, I received a response to my letter to DTE, the local electric company, regarding a downed power line in my yard and driveway. The high power had burned the yard to the dirt for about sixty feet and six inches wide. The worst of the damage was to the concrete driveway. The electricity had melted two holes in the driveway that went completely through the cement to the gravel base! I sent a letter asking DTE to accept responsibility for the damage. Their initial response to me was a short, blunt letter written as though it was from a legal mediation authority, but it was signed by a DTE bureaucrat masquerading as a competent authority.

Their next response to me was a long, convoluted letter explaining that they were not responsible because one of their subcontractors had caused the line to fall, but they are not at liberty to divulge the name of the subcontractor. We are now fifteen months into this disagreement, but I will summarize by saying that the electric company had a lawyer handling the initial complaint. They bought the word-crafter so he could run roughshod over customers with his legalistic language and implied threats. I suspect that he had either failed the Bar or has been disbarred and this was an available job for which he was prepared. My intent is to pursue this complaint until I get a fair resolution. If my electrical service was to be interrupted, I wish that it had been distributed by a small business...this would all have been resolved with a face-to-face and a handshake! Absent the legal distortions and lack of accepting responsibility, small businesses will try first to fix the problem and to save the relationship with the customer. Lawyers simply convolute that simple process and justify their wages with the fog of their advocacy, all at the expense of justice.

Large companies are more capable of marketing and defending themselves in the legal world, but then, they routinely work on their influence posture with the elected officials. I am aware of a very convoluted case where a major defense contractor was able to quietly and anonymously *seed* a government requirements office with their own engineers. The requirements were then written to fit the contractor's product and thereby eliminated many other competitors from the opportunity. One can smell the distinct odor of "justice for the well represented" in this case.

More importantly, we the people may not have bought the best product and the best price for our needs. When the whistle was blown, the lawyers came out of the woodwork and began the damage control work. They were good. The entire thing was a burp in history within a month! These things don't happen without lawyers...

Imagine a business environment where the antithesis of caveat emptor prevails where buyers and sellers openly speak, agree, and remain friends...no lawyers, no fine print, no speed talkers...just men of mutual respect. That's justice and I'll *stand* for that!

6

INSURANCE, BANKING, AND INVESTMENTS

A Modern-Day Den of Robbers Where Justice Must be Bought

The insurance and banking industries are equally infected with lawyers, both in the business and in the legal departments. I do not equate insurance and fair nor do I equate banking and fair. It's like expecting to routinely win against the house in Las Vegas. At least in Vegas, they entertain you while you pay! Have you ever actually read and comprehended the fine print of an insurance or banking document? Probably not. That is, until there is an issue, and at which time you will hear all the "obvious" reasons that you are now in the swamp and have no way out. Insurance companies delay, deny, litigate, delay, and settle in that order. Your situation or fairness does not fit into the equation.

I recently had some property damage to my house in Florida after a hurricane. I called my insurance company who denied the claim because I was not covered for that level of wind! Apparently, there is a wind matrix in the tiny print that says when at what wind speed I run out of insurance! Others tell stories of having filed a claim and then having their policies cancelled for minor and avoidable reasons after the hurricane. The financial aftermath of a hurricane is more devastating than the wind and water. Unfortunately, there are no negotiations with the insurance companies. However, there are billboard signs that advertise legal services for insurance settlements as the result of Hurricane Michael. Now you have to hire a lawyer to fight with the insurance company's lawyers with cases all filed in a court of lawyers. Meantime, the poor homeowner is living in a tent and watching his meager insurance settlement dwindle away...before he gets a dime.

About twenty years ago, a couple, then in their mid-seventies, bought a very pricy long-term care insurance policy. Ten years later, without any claims and no medical issues pending, their policy was cancelled. This after an investment of tens of thousands of dollars! They asked for help and the best that they could get (after all the fine print was explained) was that their automatic deduction expired at the ten-year mark and required them to contact the insurance company and re-institute the deduction *or* the policy would be cancelled for non-payment.

One of the folks did, in time, require long-term care, which was paid for with his savings and other family support. The insurance company essentially absconded with money these folks paid into a policy that was designed from the beginning to simply be transferred money from a geriatric couple into the corporate coffers.

But there it was in the convoluted language of the lawyers and in very tiny print…essentially caveat emptor, old folks.

Bankers are no different. Ask your banker or investment broker just who will mediate any difference between you and the banker/investment firm. You will find (after much of the crafted verbiage is deciphered) that a panel of three lawyers who are paid for by the banks/ investment firms will decide if you have a valid claim or if their employers have the better case. Who in the world would agree to such a bizarre notion? Who would write such a policy? Lawyers, of course! And why do we agree to terms that we don't or can't read? If enough of us refused to buy the insurance or take the loan or invest our money until the terms were clear in plain English, maybe the picture would change! Whose responsibility is it for this change to become effective? We have legislation in place that is intended to protect the public. Remember who crafted the legislation, who influenced it, and who voted on it? Way too many lawyers. The Federal Trade Commission is chaired by a lawyer and four of the five current commissioners are lawyers. Director of the subordinate Bureau of Consumer Protection is a lawyer.

I suspect that if I drilled down on all these lawyers that I would find that they are recycled from private practice in the field of trade, big business, maybe congress as staffers or members, and back to the FTC. Where in this vicious cycling is justice for the consumer found? Who reviews the organization and process?

Insurance and banking need to be controlled and overseen for sure. Today they are overseen by agencies established by congress, funded by congress, and whose polices are guided by congress. The same congress that is disproportionately populated by...lawyers; a congress who is the velvet glove manipulated by the hand of the lobbyists who are disproportionately...lawyers.

We have perhaps 1.2 million lawyers in this country and nearly half of them are not in the courtroom. We are being choked to death by this rising scourge on our society. Chief Justice Warren Burger forewarned us decades ago. He said that we were turning into "a society overrun by hordes of lawyers, hungry as locusts."

Following the historic Hurricane Michael, lawyers descended upon the town in droves all promising quick settlements. What I found were thieves in suits focused on their own profits. Who is standing up for the poor, unadvised, and overwhelmed victims of these disastrous events and the bureaucratic standoff that follows? As I travelled the panhandle area of Florida, I talked with dozens of our fellow Americans who simply were overwhelmed and focused on just basic survival... four months after the storm. Their misery should not result in another's profit. Their future should not be restricted by the money grab of insurance companies or lawyers.

Those who are most offended in these markets are the ones who can least afford the price of justice! I'll kneel with them.

7

LAW ENFORCEMENT

The Front Line of Justice...or Not

Law enforcement starts with the senior official being the Attorney General of the United States. Recently, we have had one AG held in contempt of Congress (albeit without any punishment); one AG who demonstrated tainted leadership in terms of witness tampering, bias prosecution (or lack thereof), and heavy handed administration of the FBI; and one AG who seemed to be frozen to inaction and ham-strung by his own declaration of recusal. Then we had an assistant AG who was stonewalling Congress and flaunting his success...without any repercussion.

The FBI itself, once the most revered and respected law enforcement agency in the world has been reduced to tatters by the horrendous actions of a significant number of the senior leadership team…all lawyers! A recent FBI Director has repeatedly perjured himself and cast a dark shadow on the integrity of the FBI. He has held many positions in law enforcement prior to his becoming the FBI Director and apparently has left a swath of malfeasance in his trail.

The FBI holds individual Americans to a very high threshold of cooperation and honesty…one which is not maintained by the FBI itself. As Congress has exercised its oversight duties, the FBI has stonewalled the production of required documents and witnesses repeatedly. If an individual citizen were to do that to the FBI or IRS, they would be met at their front door with agents with guns and handcuffs. The FBI is simply out of control. Perhaps Congress should defund the agency for a period of two years and see who or what shakes out! The number of senior Justice Department and FBI leaders caught up in the scandal of partisanship and errant investigations is overwhelming!

I am unaware of any action in the history of this nation where the survival of the republic has been put to such risk by threats from within. The demonstrably diseased Department of Justice and the FBI have lost the confidence of too many of the American citizens to continue under this leadership. The pundits all sing the praises for the working level FBI agents, but remember that leadership sets the example and the tolerance in an organization. There is no doubt in my mind that this disease has permeated, in some cases, all the way down the ranks to the newest agent in the field. I would suggest that the first tell-tale sign of a diseased local office will be an unwarranted arrogance and an "untouchable" attitude. If this were a military command, it would quickly be deemed not combat ready and pulled off the line. What appears to be the common thread, other than just plain criminality, is that they are predominantly lawyers!

In fairness to law enforcement officials, they are directed by higher authority in terms of law, policy, and resources, but the execution is their responsibility. Leadership of the law enforcement team will set the example for the department to follow. Where we jump off the rails is when the prosecution manipulates the departments to execute their agenda. For example, look at the charges brought by the Special Counsel Robert Mueller. These charges have the odor of an investigation into people in search of a crime. Lying to law enforcement, courts, Congress has proven to be a ripe target upon which to hang the charges. I looked at some of the individual charges and absent the names, they could have been a story of a prosecutor pursuing his targets by withholding information (failure to tell the whole truth); "flipping" witnesses (witness tampering); and weaving stories from a few facts (lying). This is not justice. This is lawyers acting like…lawyers.

Local law enforcement is not much better. In my small community, the county prosecutor is a loose cannon and reports to no one. He has jumped in line to assume the seat of a retiring judge just as his predecessor did…a lawyer who has been under a dark cloud of suspicion after a murder trial where there were too many questions about the conduct of the trial left unanswered. Those questions all had to do with the conduct of the officers of the court...all lawyers. Where is the justice for the accused? He rots away in prison while the lawyers vacation in the Caribbean. Do we as a society care that Lady Justice has become sighted and biased? If we care, what are our duties to correct the problems? Who leads this effort? Do we have reason to fear retaliation from the justice system? Ask Lt. Gen. Mike Flynn or George Papadopoulos! These are just a couple of examples of high level, well-funded, well-educated, and well-represented people.

Imagine how a kid from the poor side of town, represented by a public defender, and with little influence in the community, fears what the system can do to him? It's no wonder there are so many guilty pleas! A plea bargain may result in a jail sentence, but that's better than to live for a year in the fear of the justice system. I would submit that in jail, you may be safer in the long run than to risk what the system has in mind. That is just not right and I'll kneel for that!

Consider the plight of Ms. Alice Johnson to whom the President granted a commutation of a life sentence for drug trafficking. She was found guilty and sentenced as a first-time, non-violent criminal. She opted to plead not guilty where her co-defendants chose to plead guilty and take short-term sentences. Ms. Johnson stood up to the system...as was her right to do...and was severely punished for doing so. If you have any doubt about the grist mill of justice, this case should give you reason to now distrust that gristmill and demand that justice be for all, all the time.

While we are on the topic of Law Enforcement let me echo a concern voiced by a large community of recreational boaters. In 1791, the Constitution was amended and one of the amendments was the Fourth Amendment, making unwarranted searches of you and your house a violation of your constitutional rights. Over the years, the Courts have defined some exceptions for things like exigent circumstances, border searches, and motor vehicle searches, but so far, no court has touched the invasion of your home!

Now comes the modern recreational boater who is living on his boat and traveling the waterways in pursuit of happiness. These boaters can be boarded by everyone from the local "skeeter beater" to the Coast Guard who can look throughout your boat, your "home"…nothing is private and you have no rights. This is because of the Revenue Service Act of 1790, which originally sought to gain control of the inbound shipping and ensure that all tariffs and taxes were collected.

As the nation grew and changed, the Revenue Service Act did not. Recreational boaters…about 75 million strong…report having been boarded at night, in a marina, by Coast Guardsmen bearing assault-style weapons. The various boater blogs are alive with stories of multiple boardings in a short period of time, obvious "training" boardings, inappropriate searches through clothing and staterooms. Granted, most boardings are not so extreme, but the law does permit them nonetheless. If the FBI can jump off the rails so fast and become so reckless in the application of the law, what should give us comfort that the Coast Guard or any other law enforcement agency will not do the same with recreational boaters, especially those who are actually living aboard their vessel? Can you imagine being awakened by the noise of a boarding party on the deck and the pounding on the hull in the middle of the night? Then having your boat… your home…sorted through while you sit in your pajamas like an errant school boy. In the end, these American citizens… about a quarter of the US population…who have taken to the waterways to pursue their happiness, are now at risk for a very unpleasant encounter based on the interpretation of a two-hundred-year-old law by…lawyers? I have no faith that this current course of action has a happy ending! Live-aboard boaters should enjoy the same Fourth Amendment rights as homeowners.

Police academies used to teach recruits that the image of the department was built one citizen at a time and often during a roadside stop. People understand when they are wrong and are usually willing to accept the report of the offense (not a judgment) from an officer. Obviously, there are errant citizens who just take leave of their wits when stopped, but where things go wrong for the police are where the officer presents himself as judgmental and disrespectful. I have a very good driving record over my fifty-five years of driving, so when I was stopped on a small bridge in Princeton NJ by an officer who was dressed like he was on his way to invade Poland, I was stunned. He was snarky and disrespectful and informed me that I had too many veteran decals and that my VFW license plate frame blocked too much of the license plate, and he couldn't tell which state had issued the plate. There was no traffic violation, just this over-zealous, liberal-leaning officer who actually besmirched his entire community with his actions.

My point here is that a street-level cop felt comfortable being a bully. Someone gave him the impression that such behavior was okay. Law enforcement leadership does not end with graduation from the academy. Leadership in law enforcement is tough and demands that the best of the best move up the ranks. If you look closely at the leadership in police departments, you will find that the lawyers are metastasizing to the department leadership positions. Police departments need to be led by policemen...real cops who have been on the street.

I've never heard a cop say that their department is perfect, but I have heard politicians and courts defend their departments as though they were. Case in point is the shooting of a young man in Chicago by a cop. We have all seen the video of that shooting. There is just no way to see how the cop felt an immediate threat and there is no way to justify seventeen shots to his body. A follow-up investigation concluded much the same and a jury convicted the now-ex-cop of murder. The judge sentenced this ex-cop to less than seven years. How can this be viewed as a just outcome for the young man or his family? I understand that the young man was being pursued for his ill deeds and was not a pillar of the community, but at that point in time that he was shot, he was an innocent young American. How did this judge (a lawyer in a robe) summon the audacity to ignore the facts, offend the citizens and this man's family, and issue such a sentence? How can Chicago residents find equal justice for all in this sentence?

This is a judge who has self-qualified for a career elsewhere. I won't demean the people who work hard at tough, low-paying jobs by suggesting that the judge should work with them...he would be unacceptable to be on the same job as them.

When we are in danger and in need of help and protection, we know to run toward that badge...that's a sign that we're safe. When we've wronged society, we expect to be held accountable and know that the same badge will represent justice. Without equal justice, there is no justice and I'll kneel for that.

8

JUSTICE

*Equal Justice for All. Four Short Words
That Should be in the Oaths, Promises,
Commitments, and Prayers of all Those
Who Serve in the Justice System*

Our justice system is a most precious and delicate system but it has been infected with the legal locust as well. Justice is for sale…bring cash and your titles to assets. We certainly don't hear from the courts about any problems, but society cries out in many forms every day. The idiocy of the NFL and the kneeling thing is just an inappropriate distraction from the real problem—we have a part of our society that feels as though they don't get justice from our justice system. Even the perception of injustice must be addressed. But there is more than just a perception of injustice. I have witnessed the actual injustice repeatedly. I understand that the courts are busy, but they have allowed themselves to become a gristmill for the cases that are considered as being without social significance. The poor, the unrepresented or the underrepresented, those who speak English as a second language, and those whose families simply are unable to assist them become fodder for the bureaucratic brawl. Those are the souls that can't afford the cost of the adversarial system...not just the representation of the court-appointed lawyer but the win of a wordsmith.

Yes, the problem is bigger than just the perception of injustice and true injustice is at the core of it! I understand that there are a disproportionate number of blacks and Hispanics involved in crime, and I also understand that there are social threads to follow to determine why and then change the behavior, but let's stay focused on what happens in the justice system and how that undermines our good social program intentions! Go visit a courtroom and watch the practice of "justice is best for those who can influence it" in action. It will tear your heart out. How many times have you heard that our founders intended "with liberty and justice for the well represented"...never? Nor should our justice system provide for anything short of what the pledge of allegiance says, "And justice for all."

I have lived a blessed and fortunate life, but recently, I have seen just how ugly our justice system has become and at the root of the injustice is untruthfulness. I sat in a court room recently and listened to a young assistant prosecutor present her case. I was stunned by the blatant lies and the court's tolerance for her "aggressive summary." I knew from personal account that many of the statements that she presented as facts were not true and that the court and the defense knew or should have known that these were untruths, yet they stood mute and essentially suborned perjury. This young lady spun a summary from a few facts and a few creations to persuade the court that she was the winner. She won, the defendant lost, and the real Lady Justice cried beneath her blindfold.

About a year later, I was discussing this case with a local lawyer who agreed that the errant young lawyer was an over-the-top zealot, but he thought that she was beginning to "tone it down." That's good, but it didn't help a year's worth of victims of her dishonesty...and the courts' tolerance for the dishonesty! There was no justice there! In another case, I heard a judge declare, "There is no room in my court for what's right!" He was lashing out at a response to his question as to why the defendant took the action that he did. The response was "because it was the right thing to do."

I'm certain that the judge regrets his momentary release of cerebral flatulence but it does belie where his mind is in the courtroom...only the law as he interprets it, not what's right or even just. An acknowledged weakness of the adversarial system is that judges may be discovered to be out-of-touch with their community values as they tend to their monocular vision of the proceedings. This is just such a case.

Lies in court are commonplace, and responsibility for the profusion of the lies is exacerbated by the courts' tolerance for word-crafting, aggressive advocating, interpretation, and spin. Lawyers lie. As a witness in court, you cannot spin your testimony lest you risk being held responsible for not telling the court the truth. Go get a law license and your spin will be tolerated!

Those voices who cry for justice will only get louder as more citizens become aware of just how bad the system is. We must ensure that "justice for all" is, in fact, justice for everyone regardless of their social, racial, or financial status. Lawyers are the greatest impediment to justice and lawyers present the greatest threat to our society today in terms of people feeling safe...from the government!

On one of my visits to the courtroom, I listened to a case of a young lady who was standing before the judge. She was shackled hand and foot with a chain nearly as heavy as her own body weight! Her baggy, orange jumpsuit and disheveled personal appearance, along with the towering officer holding her by the arm led me to believe that I was about to learn of a horrific capital crime committed by this hardened felon who was clearly a deadly menace to society.

The judge began the very mechanical process of speed-reading the necessary charges, rights, and plea information and I was stunned that this tiny woman was being hoisted to the yardarms for being delinquent in her restitution payment to the court of $100. The judge was livid that this young lady had prioritized her expenditures as food, rent, and utilities ahead of restitution to the court. She had three small children and was a single parent.

In exasperation, the girl tried to defend her decision by saying that she was working, caring for her kids, and trying hard to make the court payments and that going to jail would mean the children would be going to foster homes and that she would lose her job and her employer would lose an employee.

The judge screeched as if she had been hit with a cattle prod and shouted that she didn't care about employment in the county and that her kids would be held by competent authorities until she completed her sentence! This was just a show of power.

The judge was *not* reflecting the mores and values of the community. She was showing that she was a tough guy and had the power to do as she wished. The tiny woman was dragged away as she pleaded for mercy. It was a scene right out of a late medieval period play. There was not a dry eye in the courtroom. This judge needs to go (as of the final edit of this book, this judge has resigned in advance of the finding of a judicial investigation)!

This is not an isolated case in America. This is repeated thousands of times a day across the nation. These cases are victims of the adversarial system's weakness for knowing and applying the reality and mores of the community. They certainly don't provide for justice! That's just wrong and I'll kneel for that.

One situation that deserves a bit more time is that which deals with people's fears of the police and the courts. Our justice system has run so far amuck that too many people are regulated by fear and not respect. I've heard the counter to this, but my personal experience across many agencies, courts, and police departments says that fear and no respect is all too prevalent. Once society turns the law over to lawyers, justice is no longer available...except to those with power, influence, or money.

Our FBI is a case in point. Our FISA courts are another example. If you look at those cases closely, you will find two distinct traits common with less-notable examples but similar in nature nonetheless...we trusted lawyers with the law; we abrogated our own civic duties and let the lawyers run away with the legal system. This falls on us, as does the responsibility for correcting the problem!

A common thread in these stories seems to be that there is some level of fear and confusion that prevents the accused from responding fully. I certainly understand this after having spent so many days observing the courts in action. The fear of reprisal by the courts, the government, or the police is simply an unacceptable situation. As I write this, I fully understand that I will suffer retribution from the local courts. I fear that.

I have watched and listened to the arguments for whether the President should be interviewed by the Special Council or not. My interest was not in the legal strategizing. I was captivated, as frozen in fear, that a frequent notion mentioned was that the President would be vulnerable to trick questions and a technique of entrapment. If that is a risk for a well-educated, experienced, worldly, and well-represented person, what are the odds for a scared kid from a disadvantaged background? That is not justice and I'll kneel for that!

As I considered and theoretically applied the proposed out-comes of that potential interview with the President, I thought of all the people of all backgrounds and social status who have been raked over the coals by over-zealous IRS agents, EPA agents, FBI agents, US attorneys, and a multitude of other government representatives using similar tactics. Prosecutions, recoveries, and investigative leads all become suspect to me. Telling the truth can land you in jail given the authorities' demonstrated propensity to…*lie*!

Flipping witnesses is another tactic that even the attorneys openly discuss with disdain. Prosecutors want the testimony of a witness and are willing to threaten, coerce, bargain, and trade to get the testimony that they want in order to secure the con-viction of their target. This testimony is often suspected to have been fabricated by the person "flipped" in order to meet the demands of the over-zealous prosecutor. The prosecutor wants the witness to "sing" and it's okay if they compose a little as well…it's all about the conviction statistics…the wins. Please understand that as an accused pleads guilty, he waives his right to a trial *and*, therefore, his right to have the government prove their case! Absent a trial, the government is free to bluster, pos-ture, and…lie to encourage a bit of composition and singing. Just for contrast, if the defendant attempts to talk with wit-nesses in an effort to get them to present a favorable testimony, they will risk charges of witness tampering! Lawyers are men of words…twisted, convoluted, self-serving contortions of what might have been the truth at some point in time. Yep, they are men of those words!

Across our nation, we have people who fear the police, some with reason, and some without reason. A person in fear does not rationalize that society is good and will protect them; people fear, and that fear is real in their minds. They fear without respect. It causes me great personal pain to think of the everyday citizens who find themselves fearing the government and law enforcement, but I believe and understand that they have reason to feel that way. That's just plain wrong and I'll kneel for that.

I have a friend who is retired from the NFL. An all-pro defensive end…a very large man! I asked him one time what his thoughts were when the blue lights came on behind him. After a little superficial machismo, he admitted that he felt fear. I suspected that would be his answer, but was struck by his rationale. Being a minority was not the issue. Being a very physical and thereby potentially threatening man, my friend feared being shot as a precaution to his becoming violent. I asked how he handled his interactions with police. His response was "with respect and a big smile!"

I applaud his technique, but it pains me to know that this wonderful Christian man first fears the police. I'm not aware of his having even minor traffic violations over the years! He is a model citizen, a model husband and father, and I am immensely proud to be his friend, so the pain that I feel for him is very personal. I can also say that he stands tall for the national anthem… all six feet seven inches of this giant standing proudly for our nation…and I am proud to stand with him anytime, anyplace!

I had the unique opportunity to work briefly with the police department in Elkhart, Indiana, and I observed the interaction between the police and the population. It's different there! The goals and objectives of the department are focused on their citizens. They had a prosecutor who set the stage for ethical law enforcement, police leadership who trained and led with integrity, and a morally strong department of officers who were citizen warriors who protected their community. It can be done…and is being done in many locales across the nation just like in Elkhart. The problem is that it is not being done everywhere. Juxtapose an Elkhart policeman to the Princeton thug I mentioned earlier. That is the stark contrast of good and bad in law enforcement!

No American should fear law enforcement. Nor should we ever feel bullied by law enforcement. We should trust them with our security and our lives. If we don't, then we should make our demands known at town hall meetings, city council meetings and finally at the ballot box. Thugs with a badge are just criminals. Analyzing the root causes of bad behavior of bad cops is just like analyzing bad behavior of criminals…there are many threads leading to the resulting behavior.

I will suggest that part of the bad behavior is precedence, perceived or real, created by the senior leadership in the law enforcement departments. That senior leadership starts with prosecutors, judges, and lawyers in the courtroom. When a young officer witnesses the bounds of untruthfulness tolerated in the courtroom, he will cater to that tolerance. His arrests will be a reflection of what the department senior leadership tolerates, what the prosecutors tolerates (or demands!), and what the court will tolerate. It doesn't take much for this snowball to gain momentum and that's from where the street abuses begin! Police academies don't teach word crafting and fact management! A young officer is prepared to report what he heard, what he saw, and what he knows to be a fact...remember, "The facts ma'am, just the facts"? Lawyers spoil that training in a very short period of time.

Prosecutors and judges who look the other way as they accrue their statistics for reelection are no better and need to be booted out as well. We need a comprehensive review of the performance standards and success measurement in a way that results in ensuring justice in all aspects of the justice system... police, prosecution, judicial, probation, and incarceration. Performance standards need to address actions required to improve society. A prosecutor's record of 99 percent conviction means nothing if those crimes charged and convicted are not what are important to the community. Staged probation violations are routinely used to fluff-up the stats. Most probation violations are easy targets...these are often our most vulnerable and least capable of defending themselves.

By the way, can you imagine judges and prosecutors being granted absolute immunity from civil suits while doing their jobs...even if the "error" committed is a terrible but easily avoidable mistake and has horrendous ramifications for the injured party? These lawyers are immune from being held responsible!

Well, accept it...our legislators (disproportionately lawyers, advised by staffers and lobbyists who are also disproportionately lawyers) passed laws that protect those in the justice system with "absolute" immunity! Doctors are held strictly responsible and must pay exorbitant insurance fees as a result (a situation created by the abhorrent tort laws enacted by… lawyers). Obviously, the cost of insurance is passed along to the health insurance companies who pass the costs along to you, the patient! The profits are realized by the lawyers and the insurance companies! School teachers are held responsible for everything imaginable. They are held responsible for hurting a child's feelings! These are for the most part people who not only have a special love for kids, they have a special drive to see kids succeed. The strict adherence to "the rules" has hampered the teaching styles and creativity of our very talented teachers in America.

A military commander is held responsible for "everything his command does or fails to do"! Commanders are often relieved of their command (fired) due to the senior commander's "loss of confidence" in the subordinate's leadership. Neither a judge nor a prosecutor comes anywhere near that kind of responsibility, authority, or accountability, yet they are granted absolute immunity. Very few things in life should be absolute…most of those would be in the domain of math, science, or religion but certainly not by or for self-serving and self-declared law gods!

Consider the reputation of a member of the Russian Collusion Special Prosecutor's office, Andrew Weissman. Here is an attorney who has collected the adoration of many fellow attorneys as a tough, hard, no-nonsense attorney, investigator, and prosecutor. But for as many who sing his praises, there are an equal number who condemn his aggressive style at achieving wins at the expense of justice. He seems to have left a swath of social carnage created by his actions many of which were reviewed and overturned by higher courts. A court reversal to a man who has served a year in prison is certainly welcome, but it will never return the lost year of his life. Yet, Mr. Weissman not only remains untouched by the error in his professional behavior, he has been rewarded with a rising career in the Department of Justice! The only absolute in this case is that Mr. Weissman should absolutely be held accountable for his malpractice before the courts and his failure to meet the expectations of the American people for "justice for all." The Bar is absolutely mute on this one!

There is an appellate process of different contortions depending on the court and the case, but in the end, lawyers govern the entire process. We need an interrupting action whereby a non-judicial panel could review a case to be certain that it is conforming to the mores and values of the community and have equal authority to reverse a decision as an appellate court. Appeals usually have to be based on a legal failure of the court or an unusually unrealistic sentence. The community review would decide if the judge has considered the local mores and values. Remember the young lady that I mentioned earlier that was sentenced to jail for failure to make a payment to the court? The community would view that much differently, I'm sure. Keeping the young lady at work and keeping the children in the family home would prevail over the payment to the court for a fine! Lastly, the entire notion of absolute immunity *must* be absolved from the books…we are *all* responsible for our actions and/or inactions!

Even the self-declared gods in robes need to be held responsible. When the judges push back, they have self-identified themselves as candidates for private practice…throw the bums out! Judges' candidacy for re-election is often a solo race…unopposed. Local lawyers fear retaliation from the judge and are unable to mount a campaign to the people. So we wait for the old goats to die. Also, we the people fail to look carefully at the judges and we either skip the vote for judges or just pick one at random. In my small community, we have six judges that serve the district at two levels of responsibility. One of the six is certifiable (bat shit crazy). Her court could be humorous if not for the fact that these are real people with whom she is toying. The Chief Judge is a former prosecutor and has long lost the ability to see justice. Three of the remaining four are average or above average. The last one is flirting with the threshold of dementia. Yet, in recent elections, they have all run unopposed.

Various States address judgeships differently. Some rely on appointments rather than elections and that brings some political baggage with it. Term limitation is another consideration, although we don't want to throw the baby out with the bath water here. The judiciary is a specialty within the legal profession and we certainly want to cultivate judges through levels of courts to ensure that we are getting the best possible judicial talent in the highest levels of courts. Perhaps a review board made up of community members should be created to review the credentials of candidates running for judgeships for reelection/re-appointment and certify them before they can be put on the ballot or reappointed.

In that manner, a bad judge would be neutered from retaliation in the courtroom and more attorneys would available to compete for the judgeships. Nothing like the bright sunshine on the process will make a more positive difference. To make the review boards standard, perhaps a state-wide process should be developed in each state. Now the phrase "throw the bums out" has some teeth!

Four short words..."equal justice for all" are perhaps the least trusted words in America by those Americans who most rely on justice without purchase. I'll kneel with them.

9

CONCLUSION

Lawyers: Stand, Face the People, and Accept Your Sentence

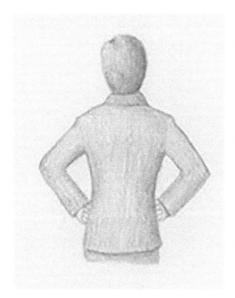

Let's review the general thesis put forward. Our major societal activities are plagued with problems that arise from unethical behavior and untruthfulness. At least, anecdotally, lawyers comprise a disproportionate number of the leadership positions in those activities. Personal observation will confirm that lawyers lie with the grace and finesse of a snake sensing its target…if their tongue is a'wagging, they're a'lying! Yup, lawyers lead the path of untruthfulness. Their conflict with their own misguided professional standards of confidentiality and zealous advocacy place them in a position to justify how they weave untrue stories from statements that are true... *lie*. Lawyers lie!

The next question is why they lie. We ultimately have to get to the goal of changing their behavior. But first, let's try to understand why they lie. Lawyers lie because we reward them to! Even lawyers will tell you that. "Yes, you hate us until you need us."

Let me rephrase that: "Yes, you hate us until you need access to justice, and then we will give you as much access to justice as you can afford...by doing whatever it takes."

As a society, we are wrong for bowing to this strong-arm tactic. We have permitted the lawyers to take over law-making (where they have created an advantage for themselves), law enforcement as they relate to the prosecutor/attorney general, and too many seats in the many societal activities that surround our daily lives. Lawyers are talkers for sure, and we hire them too often because their speech is impressive and because their speech often steam-rolls us! And all that says that lawyers lie because we reward them to! It's just that simple.

In an essay entitled "Lawyers in Character and Lawyers in Role," Katherine R. Kruse said, "Why the legal profession might be plagued with excessive lawyerly zeal that diverts lawyers away from the multiple dimensions of clients' problems and larger questions of justice: winning at all costs serves the financial and reputational interests of lawyers."

Let me state again: "Lawyers lie because we reward them to!"

In a local case of DUI, a law firm offered three levels of defense...essentially the defendant could "buy down" the punishment by paying fees increasing in $5,000 increments. Implied was that if one were to pay $15,000 dollars, there would be very little obvious punishment, perhaps unsupervised probation and a fine. On the other hand, a "minimal effort" for substantially less money would surely involve a sentence of incarceration. Yup, the best justice money can buy. If the errant morality of this concept doesn't offend the legal profession and doesn't change the behavior of the lawyers, then we the people have to change it for them. The ball is really in our court because the lawyers will dance to the tune that we pay for.

We can and should change this paradigm of untruthfulness starting in the courts. Judges should be held responsible for truthfulness in their courts. Judges need to sit attentively and listen for word crafting that is clearly distorting the facts. The judge needs to show some courage and challenge the lawyer as to his presentation. Most courtrooms are recorded both with audio and video so a review of a "day in court" should be fairly possible. I don't know if the TV court shows, along with their shock-drama judges, have influenced real judges or if the shows are just a reflection of many judges on the bench. In either case, they are wrong.

When there is a complaint about a judge, the recordings need to be reviewed by non-lawyers to see if the general tone and tenor of the courtroom actually reflects the community's mores and values. No judicial review should ever take place without a panel of non-lawyers in the room. Lawyers simply cannot be trusted with such an important duty. A judicial review by other lawyers is simply a cover-up in the making.

Prosecutors should be evaluated on statistically proven crime reduction and not on simple conviction rates. Crime statistics and the collection of data need to be done by a body separate from the prosecutor's office. Again, this duty is too important to trust to the lawyers. They will lie. The statistics should be made public on a regular basis so the public can evaluate if the prosecutor is doing the job that he was elected to do. As a matter of fairness, the statistics should be compared to other venues across the county and state, and then against the national average for similar demographic venues. Prosecutors cannot be entrusted with compiling these reports! Remember the earlier mention of my father's saying that, "Liars can figure and figures can lie, it's up to good men to be sure that they don't!" Again, we the people are those "good men"!

John Humbach wrote in his article "The National Association of Honest Lawyers: An Essay on Honesty, Lawyer Honesty, and Public Trust in the Legal System" that "our basic civic order relies on the legal system and public respect for it. If the public cannot trust the lawyers who are entrusted with the legal system, there is a problem that casts a shadow on the integrity of the very concept of rule of law."

The nation is crying in many forums for the shadow cast upon our justice system by over-zealous, misdirected (lying) lawyers! Again, I disagree with the NFL players' choice of how to voice their cry for justice, but I believe that the cry is valid and speaks of the shadow that Professor Humbach forewarned us of.

In the law, there is a provision for judging the exercise of care one would give an item. First, there is the level of care that an owner would give his personal item; then there is the level of care that a friend would give the same item if he borrowed it (equal to or better than the owner's care); and, last there is the care expected from someone who paid to use the item (less care than an owner would normally exercise). Maybe there is a parallel for that in the legal world regarding truthfulness.

Let's think about those who frequent the halls of justice. Judges preside over the court and should set the example of truthfulness by challenging bad behavior in the courtroom. Judges should be held to a very high and exacting level of integrity. Lawyers should be held to the same…or greater…standard of truth as is expected from the average citizen on the witness stand. That seems like a rather low bar for an attorney, but consider that an average citizen will rarely craft words into a false meaning…they might just lie outright, but they don't lie with the grace and finesse of the legal profession.

So, the attorney can mount a robust defense but cannot spin any more than the court would tolerate from a witness. Lies of any kind must not be tolerated in the courtroom but only an attentive, professional, and courageous judge will be able to control the cloaked lies of the lawyers.

Surprisingly enough, the American Bar Association in fact has included in their Model Rules of Professional Conduct, a multilevel standard of honesty for all lawyers! Essentially, they have a higher duty of candor in addressing the Court, not so honest when dealing with each other and the public, but the

Bar has reserved for itself the highest level of honesty when the lawyer is dealing with disciplinary matters before the Bar and during admissions to the Bar. As you can see the multilevel approach from the Bar serves...the Bar.

How can a lawyer's performance in court be guided by a rule that says they can deceive and hide evidence from each other but not from the court? There is a gray area between the two and lawyers take too much advantage of it. We need the truth to get justice and skirting the truth or hiding evidence will not get us to the truth and ultimate justice.

The Model Rules for Professional Conduct also address the issue of confidentiality in great detail; however, not once in section 1.6 is there mention of justice! The rules cover many important facets of client confidentiality and there are many opportunities to complete a sentence stating what the rule is with "in the best interest of justice." There is no part of the courts' duty that should supersede ensuring justice.

Remember the judge that I mentioned earlier for having declared "There is no room in my court for what's right?" Although I disagree with him, the Bar would agree with the basis of his declaration. Neither the Bar nor the law provides for doing what is "right," they both dodge the very difficult issue of discerning the precise focus of the application of the law that would ensure justice. With our current technological levels of sophistication, there is really no need for a judge...just enter the accused's name and the accusation. The computer will do the rest. That's 1984 on steroids! We have judges to make... judgments. Why would a judge not consider what is right to be an important part of his judgment? It's too hard. Being a judge is a difficult responsibility…but only if behaving as a judge and not a matrix robot!

I have watched judges use their judgment and issue decisions that warm one's heart that justice was achieved. These judges are too few and are too often criticized for being too lenient. It takes a strong judge to fend off that kind of criticism and continue with those good decisions (don't confuse compassionate and stupid as in the case of the homicidal cop who was sentenced to seven years!).

My proposed citizen's judicial board of review would recognize and reward these judges for the extra effort that they show to ensure justice for all. These judges are very special people in our society. We had a local judge (note…that is singular) who made arrangements shortly after his election, for his anonymous incarceration in jail, and then his assignment to a weekend substance abuse retreat. He wanted to know exactly what his punishments entailed. I salute his initiative.

Laws should be written so that the average person can understand them. Thou shall not kill. That's a law! Short, simple, and unambiguous. Now go pull your state law on murder and see if you can understand it. If laws were written in a short, concise manner absent the convolutions of the legal authors, perhaps the average person could read and understand the law and not need to hire a lawyer to interpret the law!

In military circles, there is a story used to exemplify a process for clear, concise order writing. Napoleon found that some of his tactical blunders were mistakes of interpretation of his orders. He decided to remedy the problem by stationing, near his desk, a junior soldier whose job it was to review the proposed orders and confirm that he understood Napoleon's intent. That's called the Rule of Napoleon's Corporal. Perhaps the knuckle-draggers can offer a tool to the wing-tippers of Congress!

Laws should be written so citizens can understand what their duty to obey is. Not a law that requires a citizen to hire a lawyer in order to understand the complexity of all the words and potential trap doors! Nor should the law be written to grant loopholes for special interests. None of that is in the interest of 'we the people' as we pursue justice for all!

Congress needs fewer lawyers (members and staffers) and more citizens. I am noticing more non-lawyers running for office and I think that bodes well for the future. We have a few former prosecutors in Congress and they have shown their value in searching for facts, questioning witnesses, and presenting their case, so I am not saying that all lawyers are bad. Congressman Gowdy from South Carolina is a particularly good example of one of those former prosecutors who was a great member of Congress, albeit, so disgusted with the swamp that he did not run for reelection…our loss! South Carolina's son will return home as an honorable man having served his country in the way that the Founding Fathers envisioned.

While working on this book, I was struck by the very obvious conflict of interest that exists between the Bar and the American justice system. Each State provides for the relationship of their lawyers to a Bar. Each has its own requirements for what is required to represent clients. Generally, though, to practice law, one must pass the Bar exam and be a member of the Bar (dues!). In theory, the Bar will exercise perhaps the most important aspect of a professional organization…that of enforcing adherence to the ethics of the profession. However, the Bar, and specifically the American Bar Association, is very active in lobbying et al. One could maybe trace dues extracted from members all the way to the lobbyists and their targets! Are these the same lawyers that serve as legislators, bureaucrats, and judges? The entire profession of law has a cloud of contempt hanging over it, but a population that is too afraid of it to do anything about it!

While we are cleaning house, we need to address concurrently the entire system of tort laws and now would be the time to take this on…with our new lawyer-reduced congress.

We need tort reform that rewards the citizens with fairness and justice not a system of lawyer compensation. Law schools need to be held accountable for the misdeeds of their graduates. It may be only a publication of the names of the schools that produce the highest percent of liars, or it might be a part of the tort reform efforts that would include the school in settlements where lawyers were responsible for unethical behavior that damaged another. Or the Bar could step up and accept the responsibility for cleaning up their despicable profession. The Bar should begin with rewriting the Model Rules for Professional Conduct where truth reigns supreme in all aspects of justice. I can envision a Model Rules for Professional Conduct that resembles the Ten Commandments. If a member of the Bar needs a paragraph to define a lie, then he needs to find another profession. The pursuit of truth will bring civility to the world of justice as well...not the fake civility that the lawyers in Congress practice when they operate under their "gentlemanly standing rules," rather, a civility that comes from trusting and being trusted.

I was more than a bit curious about how lawyers view ethics, so I reviewed several resources and found all to be essentially the same. Here is something about the American Bar.

First, in terms of a chronology the 1908 Canons of Professional Ethics were the predecessor to the current Model. After several evolutions of the Canons/Model, the Bar actually adopted the renamed guide as the Model Rules of Professional Conduct in 1983. The new Model is too vague to be of use. It does more to cover bad behavior that to guide good behavior.

A long-time friend and law professor cautioned me not to conflate ethics and morality. He is so right! There is no ethical code that can be written by a profession without ensuring first that the authors are men of good moral foundation. So please disregard my mention of a code of ethics with regards to lawyers. They have a weak and biased code because it was written by weak and biased lawyers to guide themselves through, around, and past the obstacles of morality and good civil behavior. Lawyers, like all of us, are guided by our inner strength of conscience and morality. No written code of ethics can supplant what is flawed in the mind. The first words of the Model should be "Justice through truth shall guide members in all facets of their practice of law."

But the real bottom line to all this is that we the people have failed in our own civic duties and have permitted the lawyers to take over. That's on us! Don't blame the lawyers. They simply reacted to a pressure…something akin to your sewer backing up…so, don't blame them. Fire them! Where appropriate, prosecute them! Build the public's confidence that justice is for all… equally. Cleanse the system beginning with the elections. Sweep the halls of Congress and the halls of justice and install fresh, untarnished public servants. If we want to change the behavior of public servants, we have to turn up the heat.

Most recently and with the announcement of a new Supreme Court nomination, the discussion of the Constitution is in the news. That is a good thing. Dr. Brion McClanahan, a noted historian and scholar wrote in his book entitled *The Founding Fathers*:

"The problem is that neither major American political party adheres to that Constitution; many of our elected representatives are ignorant of its text and original meaning. The only hope lies in a better educated public. Americans do not need judges, lawyers, politicians, or ivory tower academics descending to provide answers to our constitutional questions. The Founding Fathers have already done that for us. We just need to read what they said and hold the politicians in Washington accountable."

Dr. McClanahan published this in 2012, but it is as relevant today as it was then…as a matter-of-fact, it should be relevant two hundred years from now as well! There are two themes of note in this quote: too many lawyers in our Constitutional business and too few educated Americans ready to hold them accountable!

I have addressed the former as having to be corrected at the ballot box by informed voters. The latter is more complex. I looked into the study of civics in school and found a serious absence of the topic altogether and a very serious slant to the presentation where the topic was taught. Schools do not exist for the purpose of converting the students. Schools should be presenting topics in a manner so as to make students think about the topics with a basis of facts from which to work. Civics classes that are simply an extension of a political party's rhetoric are unacceptable. Wake up, America....your children are subject to political assuaging in too many classes and at all levels. Any class that questions the norm and causes students to question "why" or "why not" is good, but we can't tolerate one-sided political pictures of what is to be accepted as truth.

These notions extend through high school and the universities as well. The intent of the education system should be to teach students real facts as well as how to responsibly ask questions about "why" and "why not." But enough on education, that remains an important topic for another book. If we are to correct the political system in our country, we must do it with an educated and informed public. The question is how do we educate and inform the adult sector of our society. A knee-jerk reaction that I often hear is to require all voters to pass a test of civics. Okay, but how does that ensure that the voter understands the candidates, their positions, as well as the proposals on the ballots? Who can we the people trust to present these topics in an unbiased manner? I would propose that we certify an organization who has presented a plan of action for community adult education and administer that organization from a non-governmental organization, like the American Red Cross or other non-partisan organization of sufficient capability to take on this role. In the plan to educate, civics would be the foundation and progress through current events, political candidates, and propositions. This takes us a long way away from the thesis and solutions, but I could not complain about a problem and not offer some direction to correction!

I am certainly aware that all lawyers are neither bad people nor part of this problem, but enough of their profession is and the good need to report the bad...

"The only thing necessary for the triumph of evil is for good men to do nothing." (Edmund Burke).

Lawyers: Stand, face the people, and pledge your loyalty to the pursuit of equal justice for all...in all aspects of our society where you influence fairness. I will stand with you for that!

Now let the chickens squawk!

10

CASE STUDIES

The Foul Smell of Societal Gastroenteritis being Convulsed, Rejected, and Cast into the Public Venue

I have alluded to a number of cases which provided anecdotal evidence, but I delayed their broader discussion until now. I have four cases that I will try to outline: criminal, civil, financial, and divorce where I will present a layman's view of justice gone afoul.

A Thief in the Night

During the summer of 2010, I met with representatives of a small-boat manufacturing company based in Southern California. They built a specialty boat which, with some minor modifications, would have been a good solution for military applications of which I was aware. At the time, I owned a manufacturing company and was looking to expand the product base and focus on military contracts. Over the course of the next five to six months, we completed a deal to buy the company out and as part of the deal we would hire the former owner as a design consultant. He was a talented designer and builder but not quite as good a businessman or manager. Nothing about the deal was far from normal practice when buying a business. It became apparent shortly after they moved across country and began work with us every day that we could see that this man had a substance abuse problem.

A year into the operations under my roof, the former owner decided that he was unhappy and wanted out of the deal...after having accepted all the benefits of the deal. In fairness, he was a full-blown alcoholic and addict and undergoing all the difficulties that are attendant to that disease...not trying to get help, just always trying to find his next pill or drink. I tried all of the usual approaches and nothing was to deter him from his recreation. After one particularly uncomfortable confrontation over his inability to make it to work, perform any design work product at all, he stormed from the main office, which was ten miles from the manufacturing plant. This was on a Friday morning and I was uncomfortable that he was headed to create trouble at the plant, so I drove there and remained until I felt certain that he was not headed there. I visited the local police station and explained what had happened and asked if they could be especially watchful over the weekend. If he was going to do something spiteful, it would be directed at the plant. I was thinking that he'd drive his truck through the front showroom!

Instead, he hatched a plan to enter the plant discreetly and simply rob us. He entered the plant late on a Saturday night and backed trucks and trailers into the bays and he and his accomplices stole all the work in progress, the inventory of finished products, the inventory of materials, the customer records, and most of the tools and machinery. We did not discover the loss until Monday morning, when the first shift arrived.

The police were able to nail down the facts pretty quickly, including the statement of a neighboring police department officer who encountered the thieves at a gas station where they offered to sell him some of the stolen goods! The police chief reviewed the evidence and praised his officers for the quick and efficient gathering of the material. Later that week, my former contract employee, the thief, visited the chief and spun quite the tale. He and the chief became friends apparently. Meantime, the reports and complaints were presented to county prosecutor along with five three-inch binders of information listing serial numbers, pictures, supplier purchase orders and receipts, equipment inventory, and employee statements. However, the recommendation from the incompetent chief to the lazy prosecutor was that this was a matter of partners disagreeing on a business matter. The prosecutor gave the case a very low-level review and surmised in less than an hour that this was a case of a disgruntled employee, and therefore, a civil case.

Why would a prosecutor turn down such an obvious case?

I cannot begin to explain what this event did to our lives and the lives of our employees who were abruptly left without jobs. Suppliers became litigious and my life seemed to be one attorney meeting after another and one day in court followed by another day in court. We were fighting on multiple fronts daily. The boat company was completely out of business and all the pending work had to be sold to a competitor at pennies on the dollar. My warranty obligations had to be subbed out as well and all of that added to the debt. We could not get an insurance settlement because it had been determined to be a civil case. Our other businesses suffered as well and we had to lay off way too many employees.

But the lawyers were making lots of money! The insurance investigator was an attorney! The bank collector (his title was much more grand but he was still a collector) was an attorney! Each supplier and some customers had their attorneys. The only attorneys who claimed to be too busy to be involved were the public servant attorneys from the local prosecutor to the FBI. Fortunately for me, my wife, Rosanne, was more dogmatic than all the attorneys combined and her tenacity finally got us through the fight and eventually before a judge in district court where we were suing our insurance company. The judge took the time to read the entire case…hundreds of pages. Rosanne had prepared the documents in such an orderly and meticulous manner that nothing was left to question. After a month in the court process, two years and nearly a quarter of a million dollars in attorney fees later, a civil court judge found that the loss was attributable to an identified "thief in the night" and that the police and prosecutor were negligent in their duties and that the insurance company was liable for their policy limits. Today, four years later, the case still has not been reconsidered by the prosecutor. So again, why would a prosecutor turn down such an obvious case?

The prosecutor will tell you that such cases are very difficult and expensive to investigate and try. He could not justify using his limited resources on a case that impacted so few people. But tell that to the people who lost their jobs, the suppliers who lost their customer, and the city who lost a taxpayer. The prosecutor did not have a clue as to the value of the case. What he did understand was the potential risk to his stats! There was no justice for the victims...my company, my employees, my suppliers, my customers, and my community.

I think that the prosecutor did assess the costs, the risks, and the rewards and determined that the costs and risks were too high for the reward that he might receive. Justice was not in his equation! His reputation and the citable stats were the reward. I would submit that most prosecutors' offices are measured on metrics of dollars, simple numbers, and gross terms..."For one million dollars, the prosecutor's office prosecuted thousand people and had a 99.9% conviction rate for all crimes."

Perhaps a closer inspection of the facts will reveal that of the thousand cases, the majority were minor in nature and involved guilty pleas (remember the image of the defendant in the orange jump suit and Ms. Johnson); a huge number will be probation violations which can be as minor as a late payment; and of course, there are the full-blown trials where the court machinery grinds through the process with lots of efficiency but little justice.

Why are we not measuring the law enforcement efforts in terms of a reduction in the crime rates for the crimes that the community is most concerned about? Because to achieve those stats, the officials would have to work hard; apply intellectual rigor and require much more effort to present a case of why you should vote for the slug again! The people deserve justice in the justice system, not patronizing pats on the back from self-serving politicians. Let's separate the minor crimes from the ones that really threaten us. Let's enforce probation violations with less than the might of the prosecutor. Let's focus the chief law enforcement officer on the crimes that threaten our lives as well as our way of life.

During the probation violation hearing mentioned earlier, I heard the judge screech that she "didn't care about the local economy." She cared only about the missed payment in question. But the prosecutor and the judge got another "win" to report in November. The defendant got thirty days in jail, her kids were put into the foster system, a landlord lost a renter and had to move the personal items out at his expense, and a local company lost their employee. So many lives touched by the emotional and careless decision to stack the deck for reelection.

There you go, in a nutshell, why my life was turned upside down for three years…because the attorney-infected system supported the reelection of a spineless robot of a prosecutor.

Banks Gone Wild!

Several years ago, I was introduced to a situation where a local businessman from the financial world was being absolutely skewered by his banking community. Looking at the facts as they unraveled, I was stunned by how the financial community was infected by lawyers. I was further stunned by the relationship of the Banks and the Financial Industry Regulatory Authority (FINRA). Essentially, FINRA is a private organization that acts as a self-regulatory organization for member organizations, banks, brokerages, etc. The Securities and Exchange Commission (SEC) acts as the ultimate regulator of the securities industry including FINRA, but the lines of responsibility are somewhat blurred. Banks and brokerages have compliance officers who are usually attorneys. They can be an asset in terms of ensuring compliance with the various laws and regulations by the employees of the bank, or they can and are often used as a weapon against employees.

An overly aggressive compliance officer and the FINRA can instill unbridled fear into an employee. They have the power of one's career and livelihood. The only check valve is the integrity of the compliance officer and the judges of the FINRA. Anything less than the bright sunshine of honesty spells doom for the accused. Lawyers lie and this industry is no different. They are promoted, incentivized, and rewarded by their performance as recorded in the work statistics. Without the right oversight on the performance calculus, you soon find the same situation as with the prosecutors...how many did you try and what percent were convicted becomes how many violations did you discover and how many employees were terminated or sent to FINRA. None of these questions have anything to do with getting society where society wants to go. These examples of performance calculus are self-serving, organizationally protective, and common but not related to justice! And remember that these lawyers in the financial world brought with them the ethics, mores, values, and training of a tainted profession. If the laws that govern broker and bank behavior are so complex that we need lawyers to serve as compliance officers, then the laws are too damn complicated.

Honesty is much easier to define and abide by than a system of convoluted words and phrases intended to protect the guilty!

Consider the case of a broker who was clearly the high producer in a very large region of a very large bank. His production gave him lot of recognition, and I suspect fed an ego that was not minimal. None of that is a crime or a violation of regulations or laws…maybe irritating and disconcerting, but that becomes a leadership issue, not a legal issue. There was an obvious tension between the compliance officer and the broker that could be seen by all.

After numerous runs at making a case for discipline, the compliance officer was unable to do so, but was able to support the decision of management to reduce the brokers pay by 50 percent…using the argument that the broker's incentive pay (commission) created a situation where he was earning more than the district manager! The pay cut was a devastating blow to the broker's enthusiasm and his appeal to the main bank management's denial to reverse the decision was even worse. The broker was under a contract to work at the bank for several more years, but he felt that the bank had substantially changed his working conditions and compensation and that the contract was now null and void. He quit his job and the bank took the case to FINRA. Remember who funds FINRA? Yup, the banks, and they do not often bite the hand that feeds them as was the case in this matter. There was never a fair judicial review of the facts of the case beyond the FINRA review. Past incentives were all paid in bank stocks and the bank had tanked during the recession so the savings were all lost. Once the broker left the bank, he forfeited the stocks at pennies on the dollar. What became apparent in reviewing this case was that the entire investigation, accusation, and FINRA hearing process was conducted by lawyers…not bankers!

Where in the process was the intent of the bank management considered? This was a statistical win for the lawyers despite the loss of a great broker for the bank and the loss of a great job for the broker! The lives of the clients were all disrupted as they worked through the process of staying with the bank or the broker. But the lawyers won and that is all that mattered. The bank management had abrogated their moral responsibility to the hyenas.

Bankruptcy

The legal process of bankruptcy is certainly a responsible social requirement if we are to try to help people stay in business or to have a fresh restart. What I have learned about the bankruptcy process is a stunning revelation of lawyers at their lowest. In this case, the party filing the bankruptcy was a very successful professional married couple with four kids and the usual bills. The bankruptcy was forced by the loss of civil law suit where the plaintiff was awarded over five million dollars. The US Bankruptcy Court and the attorneys worked for months to structure the case. It was an obviously excruciating process of invasive home inventories, unscheduled home visits, budgets, restrictions on all purchases, including school tuition! It was clear that the attorneys were maneuvering to glean as much of the property and cash as could be taken before the Court saw the situation. There were several "sets" of attorneys who should have maintained a professional tension between their teams, but they appeared to be actually colluding together and just outside earshot of the Court.

One team recommended that $200,000 be set aside for taxes so the judge could see the intent to pay taxes. One team simply required cash payments when demanded, which was usually just before a motion or an answer to a motion.

I watched these folks be torn from limb to limb by these hyenas. Once the Court rendered a decision and laid down the terms of the bankruptcy, the firm that recommended the $200,000 tax set aside demanded a $200,000 final payment on their services. The Court had already approved the case and fees. This was done behind the back of the Court and had been planned that way all along. The threat to the young couple was that if they didn't like the terms, then the bankruptcy case would be reopened and the inventories, budgets, and spending restrictions would continue for another year...at least. These people caved, their will having been crushed as they looked at how to keep one child in college, one just getting into college, and two in parochial school. They could not afford another year of the process. One firm demanded $500,000 for services that were not even documented with any credibility. There was no contract for services, no work product, no evidence of anything. They had been paid several hundred thousand dollars over the years of the bankruptcy process, but this $500,000 was an ambush. The firm assigned a collection attorney from their staff that became very aggressive and demanded assets from the extended family of the young couple.

The family negotiated a settlement of some complexity with provisions for an early and deeply discounted payoff and that proved to be the only saving grace of the entire event. Again their point of leverage was that they could "throw a wrench into the bankruptcy" and send these folks back into the process again. Remember the discussion earlier about fear and intimidation? These lawyers used their legal knowledge and Bar associations to essentially blackmail the couple into an arrangement that best served the attorneys! How, in any decent society, could this be tolerated? How does the court become informed? How can one judge the Bar association strength in terms of finding a sympathetic ear in the court to hear the story without further antagonizing the Bar members…risking the further abuse of the justice system? Without integrity, truthfulness, and a reputation for such in the legal field, we the people are held hostage to their shenanigans without recourse. Now is the time to bring this to a halt.

There is much fault here on the part of the couple who suffered the event. Setting here in my office, I can find all kinds of errors of judgment and emotion, but when faced with such high stake losses that could divide the family, these folks weighed the case and paid the devil. The attorneys, on the other hand, knew what the limits were and clearly crossed those limits. They were driven by the lust for cash and were willing to throw integrity, principles, and even people to the wind to get that cash. I spoke personally with two of the attorneys in a social setting, and they both talked about the importance of strict adherence to attorney ethics and how much they deplored those attorneys who violated the special trust between an attorney and the folks who depend on them. They were convincing with sincere expressions and gestures…all part of legal theatrics 101.

The entire legal vocation should hang their head in shame with each story like this. Lawyers like this are a despicable breed of hyena. As a civilized society, we have many changes to make in how we tolerate the abuse of power from the entire legal community. This will be most challenging because of the threatened retaliation of the system and the members of the legal profession. As I write this book, I know full well that I will suffer the wrath of a vindictive, lawless, and dishonest justice system as a result of my raising these questions. I'm too old to care. This has to change or our country will face increasing risks of collapse from within.

Divorce

After thirty-nine years of marriage, my wife filed for divorce. I will not claim to have been a model husband. I was a Marine for thirty-four years and constantly deployed. My career overshadowed my family and that is on me. My wife had some mental health problems that are personal and will not be discussed other than to say that the doctors had repeatedly recommended several social changes in addition to the medications that would enhance her mental health.

She never abided with the social interaction recommendations. Medications were often found to be overlapping, conflicting, or outdated. Maintaining medication awareness was a full-time job, but I did the best that I could. In my absence, it was a hit-or-miss proposition. Paranoia, insecurity, and hostility were hallmarks of her personality. There were extreme lows but very few highs. Eventually, the grind of confrontation became too much and the divorce was a logical outcome. Her psychiatrist referred her to a local lawyer, who quickly took the case. That was essentially the last of the discussion of any mental health issues at all!

The attorney quickly organized his attack and was able to conjure up a "witness" that even my ex-wife found to be an unreliable witness! He sent over two hundred subpoenas to banks, businesses, and family demanding financial information. Most of the larger companies recognized the unenforceability of such a subpoena and simply ignored them. Others hired lawyers and responded with anger.

My attorney is an Eagle Scout! He is a friend. He is a decent, upstanding gentleman. He is completely out of his element in the murky world of deceitful lawyers. There are many lawyers like him, but they are outnumbered but those who are just the opposite of him. My ex's attorney, by contrast, was a slippery, fact-ignoring, blatantly dishonest, run-of-the-mill lawyer who you normally find slinking around the courthouse or hawking his business and passing out business cards at the hospital ER.

I was stunned by the tactical shenanigans that he performed, but more astonishingly, I was shocked by what the court tolerated. His legal modus operandi was (and remains) to overwhelm the opposition with motions, subpoenas, allegations, and delays. In court, he "stated," without admonition from the court, some of the most ludicrous things that one could imagine...he told the courtroom full of people that I owned a multibillion dollar, publicly traded, Canadian company! The judge sat mute. I was stunned. He alleged that I had taken about two million dollars from my business and was hiding it!

This was absolutely untrue and totally unsupported by facts and exactly counters the testimony of a major accounting firm's CPA who audited the books and found no evidence to support the claim. He had a private detective follow me, my employees, and my family in an effort to find something of value.

In the end, he did not call the detective as a witness nor did he submit the reports. It was month later before I was privy to why...the detective's summary was that I was a pretty boring individual who spent my time working and taking care of my daughter! The detective found no unusual behavior from any of my employees or family! The allegations of extramarital events, financial misappropriation, abuse, neglect, and business mismanagement eventually all went undocumented and unproven as they should have been. Nonetheless, the allegations were voiced in the courtroom and printed on motions. None of that made them true, but in lawyers' parlance, "If you throw a skunk in the jury box, you can't instruct the jury not to smell it."

This lawyer threw as many skunks as he could and was never challenged. It was a strategy based in untruthfulness. The court essentially suborned the untruthfulness by saying nothing. Each day, this lawyer arrived at trial with an assistant pulling a luggage cart stacked high with plastic crates of papers...probably nothing more than scrap paper but the image was what was important regardless whether it was an honest or deceitful image. Lawyers lie! With each witness, this unscrupulous lawyer "testified' as much as he inquired and the judge tolerated the attorney testimony without comment. His testimony was very theatrical and laced with innuendos, half-truths, and outright misrepresentations. The judge's catatonic presence never changed. He was simply permitting a fellow lawyer earn his money. Justice was not a part of this trial!

During a follow-on motion years later, this same attorney made similar accusations of misbehavior, neglect, and hidden assets, all without any evidence and all disproven but only because I carried the burden to prove my innocence in the face of his allegations…and no court support!

In his subpoenas, he demanded the financial records of my consulting business clients, some of which were large businesses in the defense industry. The limits of his misguided search for evidence were unbounded.

There seems to be enough substance in the Bar's own guidance to have precluded this attorney's misbehavior or at least a predicate for the judge to admonish the attorney that he had crossed the line of ethical behavior. Consider Rule 3.4(e) of the Model Rules of Professional Conduct, which states:

> A lawyer shall not:
>
> (e) in trial, allude to any matter that the lawyer does not reasonably believe is relevant or that will not be supported by admissible evidence, assert personal knowledge of facts in issue except when testifying as a witness, or state a personal opinion as to the justness of a cause, the credibility of a witness, the culpability of a civil litigant or the guilt or innocence of an accused.
>
> Rule 8.3 extends the duties of the attorneys beyond their personal conduct and

requires an independent duty to report violations of the Rule of other attorneys.

Rule 8.3: Rule 8.3 Reporting Professional Misconduct

(a) A lawyer having knowledge that another lawyer has committed a violation of the Rules of Professional Conduct that raise a substantial question as to that lawyer's honesty, trustworthiness or fitness as a lawyer in other respects, shall inform the appropriate professional authority.

(b) A lawyer having knowledge that a judge has committed a violation of applicable rules of judicial conduct that raises a substantial question as to the judge's fitness for office shall inform the appropriate authority.

I indicated a desire to appeal the bizarre finding of the court and was told after a meeting with the judge, my lawyer, and the snake that I had nothing to worry about because the judge said that he could correct everything in the next hearing. Interestingly enough, the next hearing was delayed and the new date was two days after the last date to file for an appeal!

Why did I accept that? Legal precedent as set forth in Cotto v. United States, 993 F.2d 274 (1st Cir. 1993) where the court ruled that "the government acted in a Svengali-like manner, lulling them to sleep with settlement songs while the sands of time drained and the appeal period expired."

In this case, as in most like it, the court was complicit in the abuse of justice! The court knew or should have known that the appeal clock was ticking and should have advised the principals. My case was less dramatic but followed the same illogical path of legal deviousness. I was responsible and I accept that. I trusted way too much and demanded way too little. That will never happen again!

SOCIETAL REMEDIATION

What to Do?

The purpose for the book is to generate an awareness with the readers as to how prolific the problem of unethical behavior has become in our society, and how unethical lawyer behavior seems to lead the way; but most importantly, to create a wave of public outcry for change. The current political landscape is ripe with evidential stories of what is wrong and who is at the core of the issues...lawyers. The Justice Department including the FBI is riddled with damage caused by the misbehavior and unethical behavior of lawyers and the details of that need to be exposed and published in a book.

I understand that there are authors with books in the process and I am very encouraged by that!

From my readings, I believe that the adversary system that we adhere to in our "justice" system has become exaggerated and has metastasized to other areas of our society. The rules within the adversary system have been discussed ad nauseam by legal scholars, practicing lawyers, and the judiciary. The discussion is actually very interesting, but from the laymen's point of view, it still comes down to truthfulness. I can't find the moral argument for withholding facts, contorting facts, or any of the other strategies of the profession.

I came across a phrase, "Weave stories that are false out of statements that are true…" If anyone can accept that as good, then they are part of the problem. Nonetheless, many of the cases that I reviewed and the articles and essays that I read actually praised the skill and craftiness of the lawyers who won cases based on their ability to tell an untruthful story that was strung together with some truthful facts. To be clear, this "skill" is not part of the adversary system, but it is permitted through the elastic nature of the Model Rules of the ABA. Listen to the speech of a lawyer/politician…emotionally, you like the song, but intellectually, you have to discern the disgusting distortions of the truth that he is spewing.

How did we ever allow this vile concept into our system of legislation…lawyers, that's how!

As you think back to the chapters of this book…business, insurance, banking, investments, etc., can you see where this legal elasticity has taken us? A clever crafting of words might save an insurance company money in the long run, but at what cost to the American public, our economy, and that poor soul who thought they were insured and had made all the payments over the years, only to find that a few well-crafted words left them in distress? I don't believe for a minute that in a macro view, that any decent person will agree with the elastic law that lawyers bring to our society. Even in a micro view, that is, our own personal situation, I think that we would have to agree that truthfulness outweighs the small gains we might make by being less than truthful.

Each industry has to look at themselves through moral introspection and see if they are a truthful organization or a variably truthful organization. If they can scrub their policies, practices, and contracts and report to the people that they have "come clean," I suspect that they will feel a resurgence of business. I am reminded of the TV campaigns for Wells Fargo bank and Facebook. Each got caught in the public eye behaving poorly and each ran ads appealing to the public in saying that they had looked inward, discovered things that they did not like about themselves, and were on the road to becoming a more trustworthy company in service to the American people. I suspect that neither company sniffed out the details of what took them to the corner of that dark room, but I suspect that one could find that lawyers with their convoluted policies and crafty words had much to do with it. Within months of this effort, each company was back in the news as having again violated the trust of the people who trusted them. The full recovery of these two giants will depend greatly on leadership from the top... good, solid, morally strong leadership. As of this writing, these two giants are simply waiting to be slain.

CONCLUSION

In conclusion, there are some obvious finds:

1. That too many lawyers spoil the law.
2. That there are too many ill-behaved lawyers in all aspects of society.
3. That too many lawyers define truth to be a circumstance that, with their spin, can become a fact and therefore is now a truth for which they can demand a high ransom!
4. That lawyers need a leash and a muzzle held in place by civilian review boards. If the American and State Bars cannot police their own profession, then we must police it for them. A review board of non-lawyers can fulfill that responsibility.
5. That lawyers, under their current ethics, are a scourge that threatens our freedoms and our way of life. If our businesses, politics, and justice systems continue down the road of deceit and distrust, we will become a nation of distrust...much like the former Soviet Union! Our daily lives rely on a system of justice in which the public can place their trust and confidence. If we can't trust the lawyers who run the legal system to run that

system with integrity, then we have to take the system away from their control or accept the Soviet-like darkness that will prevail over our daily lives.

6. That lawyers have carved into the laws (torts), a long-term job security program at a huge cost to "we the people."

7. That lawyers have carved into the laws a system of protection for their own incompetence, carelessness, deviousness, dishonesty, and stupidity through the absolute immunity rule. The judicial world will respond with eloquent statements of justification for their having this immunity, but I will respond to them simply by saying that we are all equally responsible for our actions and/or inactions. For the legal profession and the judiciary in particular, I would say to set the artful speech aside, do the right thing and accept responsibility for your decisions.

8. That Prof. John Humbach, in his essay "The National Association of Honest Lawyers: An Essay on Honesty, "Lawyer Honesty" and Public Trust in the Legal System" has captured the heart of the problem with his statement, "The growing public disquiet about lawyer ethics is not mainly because people think lawyers neglect their professional standards. Rather, the main problem is the belief among lawyers that the duty of loyalty to clients requires lawyer to mislead." Bingo!

My intent was never to identify problems without solutions, so here are my recommendations for corrections:

We need public education and awareness training on government! Low information voters are dangerous! Begin with all people that receive some form of public assistance...not just financial assistance, but everything from transportation to food. We need to tell these people that they are important to our government process and that they need to understand what their duties and responsibilities are as well as their rights. Make education a part of the assistance system. Let's educate voters! These classes must be apolitical!

We need to encourage more involvement in elections including more volunteers (non-lawyer) on the street in a non-partisan role to encourage and assist voters. We the people have to know that we are hearing and speaking the truth. This is an area for non-profit/volunteer leadership and experience. There are hundreds of people who would help but may need some encouragement and assistance to make the decision. The motivations can be everything from courteous asking to free meals at the event. Those with experience in this area will have a wealth of talent in establishing a program by area and demographic.

We the people must demand for swift, transparent action against public officials who have violated the public's trust and more courage from our congress lest they join the ranks of unemployed. I don't like the mass demonstrations, but they might be part of the answer. I do like organized letter and call campaigns to political leaders! Inaction on the part of a politician should be revisited during their campaign for reelection. But who tracks, leads, and follows up on the effort? We have seen the retaliation of the IRS against political activists...

I would submit that a street-level plan of action needs to be developed and made available to every community, organization, and political activist in the country. From that plan of action, there needs to be leads for funding, sample letters, Congressional points of contact, "how to" canvas, and local organization. This is a project ripe for a university to take the lead!

There needs to be a constant pressure on the Bar to do what binds a profession together...ensure that professional standards and ethics are adhered to and take punitive action taken where they are violated. This should include reviewing and rewriting the Bar's Model Rules of Professional Conduct as required.

"The bounds of the law in a given case are often difficult to ascertain." This is the epitome of elastic application of the law! Unfortunately, this effort to rewrite may have to be led by lawyers...members of the Bar. There are good lawyers out there and now is the time for them to stand up and take the profession back from the dark side.

Obviously, this was written with some tongue-in-cheek comments and certainly with some personal bias and interpretation. Those are facets of my personality and my experiences. But I believe that they are the truth and represent the facts as they exist. The bottom line is that as a society, we are well down a path of routine and accepted deceit in our daily activities and that is a disaster in the making.

I have spent much time on pointing at lawyers because I think that they have set the course and lead the way, but this is a target-rich environment if we consider the entire employed population of the media, banks, insurance companies, pharmaceutical companies, marketing companies, etc. The only way out is to squash the insects of depravity and instill the values of truthfulness and professional conduct in all of our professions. Lawyers could lead this correction or…just continue to defend their turf.

From this new societal posture of honesty, "We the People" will enjoy…justice for all!

INDEX

WORKS CITED

Humbach, John A. "Just Being a Lawyer: Reflections on the Legal Ethics of a President under Impeachment." Review of An Affair of State: The Investigation, Impeachment and Trial of President Clinton, by Richard A. Posner. *Pace Law Faculty Publications*. http://digitalcommons.pace.edu/lawfaculty/449/.

Humbach, John A. "The National Association of Honest Lawyers: An Essay on Honesty, Lawyer Honesty and Public Trust in the Legal System." Pace Law Review 20, no. 1 (September 1999): 93.

Kruise, Katherine R. "Lawyers in Character and Lawyers in Role." *Nevada Law Journal* 10, no. 2 (2010): 393.

Rifkind, Simon H. "The Lawyer's Role and Responsibility in Modern Society." *The Record* 30, (1975): 534, 543.

ACKNOWLEDGMENTS

I began this effort more as a cathartic exercise than a book. My frustration with what was happening in our society and my personal experiences seemed to intersect with the notion that too many people were simply not being honest with each other. My wife, Rosanne, encouraged me to begin the process and then encouraged me daily to capture more of the details of my frustration and write them down. She expanded her role as the COO of our business to serve as both the CEO and COO so that I could spend more time on the writing. Her encouragement was much appreciated, but her blunt honesty was absolutely needed. Her twin sister, Elizabeth Randall, a career educator, was part of that effort as well!

My sister, Dr. Mary K. Jones, herself a published author and university professor, took the time to assist me with the reading, editing, and the publishing decisions. This was all new to me, and I much appreciated the help!

Most importantly, I want to acknowledge you, the reader, for taking time to read my thoughts. I hope that I have moved you to act! Whether you are an activist, a speaker, a voter, or a neighborhood gossip, I appreciate your helping to carry the message that we can make a difference in our society if we tell the truth and hold all others responsible for their telling the truth as well…especially the lawyers!

ABOUT THE AUTHOR

Bradley M. Lott, Major General, US Marine Corps (Ret.) is CEO and owner of True North, a consulting firm in St. Clair County, Michigan, that is primarily focused on assisting businesses in Defense and Government contracting.

General Lott retired from the US Marine Corps in January 2006, after having completed 34 years in the Corps. His last Marine Corps assignment was as the Deputy Commanding General, Marine Corps Combat Development Command, Quantico, Virginia. Additionally, he served as the Marine Corps Principal Representative to the Joint Capabilities Board, which supports the Assistant Commandant of the Marine Corps and the Vice Chairman of the Joint Chiefs of Staff in carrying out their responsibilities with the Joint Requirements Oversight Council.

General Lott holds a Bachelor of Science degree from the University of West Florida and a Master of Science degree from the University of Southern California and is a graduate of the National Security Program at Harvard University. His military decorations include the Defense Superior Service Medal, Legion of Merit with gold star, Defense Meritorious Service Medal, Meritorious Service Medal, Navy and Marine Corps Commendation Medal, Army Commendation Medal, Navy and Marine Corps Achievement Medal, Combat Action Ribbon, Joint Meritorious Unit Award, Navy Unit Citation, Meritorious Unit Commendation, and he wears the Navy/Marine Corps Parachutist insignia.